TUKARAM

Tukaram

R. D. RANADE

State University of New York Press

First published in 1933 by Mr. Anant Vinayak Patwardhan, Poona, as part of the title *Indian Mysticism: Mysticism in Maharashtra.*

Published by
State University of New York Press, Albany

Printed in China

For information, address State University of New York Press, State University Plaza, Albany, N.Y., 12246

Production by Cathleen Collins
Marketing by Dana Yanulavich

10 9 8 7 6 5 4 3 2

Contents

Biographical Introduction

The Date of Tukārāma's Passing Away

1. It is an unfortunate thing that, in spite of much research, there should still be a definition about the dates of the birth and death of a celebrated saint like Tukārāma. It may be said, however, that the date of Tukārāma's passing away is a little more definite than that of his birth. In an MS. of Tukārāma's Gāthā, which is preserved at Dehū, the place of Tukārāma's birth and death, the date of his passing away is given as 1649 A.D. (Śake 1571); while in the copy of Tukārāma's Gāthā written by Bāḷājī, the son of Santājī Jaganāḍe, the famous disciple of Tukārāma, the date of Tukārāma's passing away is given as 1650 A.D. (Śake 1572). It is to be noted, however, that the date on which Tukārāma passed off is generally recognised to be Phālguna Vadya 2, Thursday. Now Phālguna Vadya 2 does not fall on Thursday in 1649 A.D. (Śake 1571), but in 1650 A.D. (Śake 1572). Hence the greater probability of 1650 A.D. (Śake 1572) being the date of Tukārāma's passing away from this life.

Theories About the Date of Tukārāma's Birth

2. As regards Tukārāma's birth, there are four different theories: (1) Mr. Rājavaḍe relying upon the entry in an MS. of the Gāthā with a Vārkarī at Vāī, fixes upon Śake 1490 (1568 A.D.) as the date of Tukārāma's birth. Moreover, he quotes an Abhaṅga of one Mahipati that Tukārāma was initiated about thirty years after Bābājī's passing away. The main argument against Rājavaḍe's date is that if we are to suppose that Tukārāma was born in 1568 A.D. (Śake 1490), he must have been eighty-two years of age at the time when he passed away, that is, in 1650 A.D. (Śake 1572), and we know that it is a historical fact that when Tukārāma died, his wife, who was only seven or eight years younger than himself, was pregnant, and that later she gave birth to Nārāyaṇa, who was thus Tukārāma's posthumous son. Now we could not ordinarily suppose that a son could be born to a man at the age of eighty-two. Hence, Mr. Rājavaḍe's date cannot be regarded as very convincing. Rājavaḍe says that if his date were to be regarded as true, then we can very well explain how Tukārāma was initiated in Śake 1520 (1598 A.D.) on Māgha Śuddha 10, which is a Thursday. (2) Mr. Bhāve argues from this date of Tukārāma's initiation, namely, Śake 1520 (1598 A.D.), Māgha Śuddha 10, which was a Thursday, backwards to about twenty-one years, when, accordingto him, Tukārāma was born, which gives us the date 1577 A.D. (Śake 1499). Bhāve thus relies upon 1598 A.D. (Śake 1520) as an absolutely reliable date of Tukārāma's initiation, and deduces all other dates from it. (3) Mr. Pāngārakar tries to prove that the famine referred to in Tukārāma's Abhaṅgas must be taken to be in 1629 A.D. (Śake 1551), and that very soon later Tukārāma was initiated, namely, in Śake 1554 (1632 A.D.) on Māgha Suddha 10, which also was a Thursday. Also, Pāngārakar relies upon Mahipati's evidence that half of Tukārāma's life had been spent before the time of the famine, and the remaining half later, from which fact he goes back twenty-one years and comes to 1608 A.D. (Śake 1530) as the date of Tukārāma's birth. Now these dates, namely, Śake 1530, 1551, 1554 as the dates of Tukārāma's birth, of the famine, and of the initiation, are not impossible ones. But it must be remembered that Pangārakar, on the evidence of Mahipati, conceives Tukārāma's life to be divided exactly into two half portions at 1551. Probably what Mahipati meant was that "about" a half of Tukārāma's life and not exactly a half was spent at the time of the famine. Moreover, it must be remembered that Mahipati lived about 125 years later than Tukārāma, and that sufficient time elapsed between the two to allow some legends to grow about the life of Tukārāma. Moreover, if we take 1608 A.D. (Śake 1530) as the date of Tukārāma's birth, Tukārāma becomes a very short-lived man, that is, he was only forty-two years of age at the time of his passing away, and thus we cannot very well explain the reference to old age जरा कर्णमुळीं सांगों आली गोष्टी in Tukārāma's Abhaṅga's except in a vicarious fashion. (4) We thus come to a fourth date as not an improbable date of Tukārāma's birth. It is 1598 A.D. (Śake 1520) as given in the family chronolgies of Tukārāma both at

Dehū and Paṇḍharapūr. Now it is true that in these chronologies it is also told that the date of birth was Māgha Śuddha 5, Thursday. Now the fact that Māgha Śuddha 5, Thursday, does not occur in 1598 A.D. (Śake 1520) must not make us suppose, as Pāngārakar says, that Śake 1520 is an impossible date. The vagaries of calculation according to the Indian almanac are proverbial. Besides, if we are to give up either 1520 or Māgha Śuddha 5, Thursday, we had rather give up the second by all means. It must be remembered, however, that this date, namely, Śake 1520, is sanctioned by the family chronologies of Tukārāma both at Dehū and Paṇḍharapūr, and that it accounts for the reference in Tukārāma's Abhaṅgas to his old age, and yet does not make Tukārāma too old at the time of his death. As to the year again, when the famine took place and when Tukārāma was initiated, as we have pointed out above, we need not go to 1629 A.D. (Śake 1551) as the only year of famine. There are famines in India every now and then, and it is not impossible that some famine near Śake 1541 would have been meant. 1632 A.D. (Śake

1554) as the date of Tukārāma's initiation could then be brought back to 1619 A.D. (Śake 1541), on which there was Thursday on Māgha Śuddha 10. It thus seems probable that Tukārāma having been born in 1598 A.D. (Śake 1520), experienced a dire famine some time before 1619 A.D. (Śake 1541), when he lost his wife and trade, became sorrow-stricken, and gave himself up to the contemplation of God, when in Śake 1541 (1619 A.D.) on Māgha Śuddha 10, Thursday, he was initited by Bābājī in a dream. Thus Tukārāma's earlier life of twenty-one years having been spent in Samsāra, the remaining thirty-one years, namely, from 1619 A.D. to 1650 A.D. (Śake 1541 to 1572) were spent in Paramārtha. Thus we can provide for a reasonably long time for the seed of Tukārāma's spiritual teaching to sprout, to flower, and to fructify. The 21 years before initiation and the 31 years after initiation do not balance against each other as half and half; but what we have to understand from Mahipati is that the life of Tukārāma was divided into two portions, the earlier and the later, the earlier having been given to worldly matters and the later to spiritual.

Incidents in the Life of Tukārāma

3. The main incidents in Tukārāma's life may now be briefly recapitulated. Tukārāma was born in 1598 A.D. (Śake 1520), and about 1613 A.D. (Śake 1535), Tukārāma was married. It is well known that he had two wives: one Rakhumābāī, and the other Jijābāī. Soon afterwards his parents died. Tukārāma suffered a loss in trade. His first wife Rakhumābāī died for want of food in a dire famine. His son named Santu also died. Tukārāma now went to Bhāmbanātha and Bhaṇḍārā and other places, and gave himself up to spiritual reading. In Śake 1541 (1619 A.D.), on Māgha Śuddha 10, Thursday, he was initiated by his Guru Bābājī in a dream. We can see how Tukārāma must have experiencd the dark night of the soul, and ultimately have come to God-vision. After having realised God, he taught others the same instruction in his Kīrtanas. He usually performed Kīrtanas at Dehū, Lohagaon and Poona. He was hated by Rāmeśvarabhatta, who, however, later became his disciple. He was also scornfully treated by Mambājī Gosāvī, who also later repented. Tukārāma's wife was a Xantippe, often quarrelled with her husband, told him that he was doing no work to maintain his family, and snarled when Tukārāma received all sorts of guests and gave himself to spiritual Kīrtanas. Tukārāma suffered all these things in patience. He continued to preach the secret of spiritual life to those who assembled around him. Before he died, Tukārāma probably met both Śivājī and Rāmadāsa. Śivājī had passed his teens at the time, and had already taken Toranā, and was trying to found a Marāthā kingdom. Tukārāma directed Śivājī to have the spiritual instruction of Rāmadāsa. Tukārāma also probably met Rāmadāsa when the latter had gone to Paṇḍharapūr to visit the temple of Viṭṭhala. Having led an intensely spiritual life, Tukārāma passed away in Śake 1572 (1650 A.D.), Phālguna Vadya 2. There is a story told that Tukārāma ascended to heaven with his body. This is to be credited only as little as or as much as the ascension of Christ. The story must have originated in the fact that there is no Samādhi of Tukārāma built anywhere. There is a Samādhi of Jñānadeva, there is a Samādhi of Rāmadāsa, there is a Samādhi of Ekanātha, there is a Samādhi of Nāmadeva, but there is no Samādhi of Tukārāma either in Dehū or at any other place. This is probably the reason why Tukārāma has been supposed to have ascended bodily to heaven. The philosophical meaning of the story seems to be that Tukārāma was liberated before death by virtue of his God-vision, or that his very body had become divine in the process of God-contemplation.

The Making of Tukārāma's Mind

4. There are a few points in the life-history of Tukārāma which we must now disentangle with some care. The question has been asked as to who exercised the greatest amount of influence in the formation of the mind of Tukārāma. In the first place, it must be noted that the direct impulse to spiritual life must have come to Tukārāma from his spiritual teacher Bābājī. There are some historical things known about Bābājī and his line. Tukārāma himself tells us that his spiritual line may be traced from Rāghava Chaitanya to Keśava Chaitanya and to Bābājī Chaitanya. Bahiṇabāī, one of Tukārāma's greatest disciples, who had seen him and had lived under his instruction, tells us that Rāghava Chaitanya was a spiritual descendant of Sachchidānanda Bābā, who was himself a disciple of Jñānadeva. From this, it may be seen that Tukārāma came directly in the spiritual line of Jñānadeva. Now, Bahiṇābāī's evidence in this respect must be considered as more authoritative than the evidence either of Niḷobā or Mahipati, as she lived in Tukārāma's presence, and Tukārāma must have probably told Bahiṇābāī that Rāghava Chaitanya was spiritually descended from Jñānadeva. Then, again, as regards the historical evidence for these Chaitanyas, there is a work called Chaitanyakathākalpataru written in 1787 A.D. (Śake 1709), and based upon another work referred to in that book by Kṛishṇadāsa in 1674 A.D. (Śake 1596), *i.e.*, only twenty-five years after the death of Tukārāma. There, we are told that Rāghava Chaitanya lived in Uttama-nagarī, that is to say, in modern Otūra, on the banks of the

Pushpavatī, known also as Kusumāvatī, which may be seen running into the river Kukadī. Rāghava Chaitanya initiated one Viśvanātha Chaitanya, and called him Keśava Chaitanya. Some people identify Keśava Chaitanya with Bābājī Chaitanya, while others say that they were two different persons. In any case, it is clear that Tukārāma mentions the name of his own spiritual teacher as Bābājī. Next in importance to the receiving of spiritual instruction from Bābājī, Tukārāma refers to four different persons as having peculiarly contributed to the formation of his spiritual life. There is a famous Abhaṅga of Tukārāma, to be uttered in tune with the sound of a Ṭiparī, where Tukārāma tells us reiteratingly चौघांची तरि घरि सोय रे —"at least follow these four." These four are, first Nāmadeva, the boy of a tailor, who played without faltering; then, Jñānadeva, who with brothers and sister danced around God; then Kabīra, the disciple of Rāmānanda, who was a worthy partner to these; and finally, Ekanātha, the child of a Brahmin, who gathered about him a number of devotees. These played, says Tukārāma, the game of spiritual life, and the game never affected them. Thus, we see, that Tukārāma calls our mind to the teachings of these four great saints, indicating probably that his own mind was specially influenced by them. We can see from the account we have given of the relation between Jñānadeva and Tukārāma in what high respects Tukārāma had held Jñānadeva. As regards Tukārāma's relation to Nāmadeva, the only meaning in the story that calls Tukārāma an incarnation of Nāmadeva is that the spiritual methods of the two were probably one. When Prof. Patwardhan says that Nāmadeva appears to put more sentiment in his Abhaṅgas, while Tukārāma surpasses him in logical consistency; that while Nāmadeva is more emotional, Tukārāma is more intellectual, we do not think that he represents the case accurately. Tukārāma is so much like Nāmadeva and both go so much by emotion, that we see that they leave no room whatsoever for philosophical argument. For that matter, we may say that Jñānadeva is more intellectual than either Nāmadeva or Tukārāma. But between Nāmadeva and Tukārāma, there is nothing to choose, so far as the life of emotion and the life of mystical experience which transcends all philosophical arguments are concerned. As regards Ekanātha, we know how Tukārāma had dived into the Bhāgavata of Ekanātha, and had committed the Bhāgavata like the Jñāneśvarī almost to memory. Thus, it is not untrue to say, as Mr. Pāngārakar has pointed out, that the Gītā, the Bhāgavata, the Jñāneśvarī, the Commentary of Ekanātha on the Bhāgavata, and the Abhaṅgas of Nāmadeva peculiarly moulded Tukārāma's spiritual life. When the influence of the thoughts of these writers was added to the spiritual instruction which he had received from his master, upon both of which he pondered in solitude, resigning his mind to God in the utterance of His name, it is no wonder that the outcome should be that of a very mature soul like Tukārāma, who not merely realised God himself, but brought God-realisation within the easy reach of all.

Tukārāma, Śivājī and Rāmadāsa

5. There is another point in the life-history of Tukārāma which is also well worth noticing, namely his meeting with

Śivājī and Rāmadāsa. If we consider carefully the dates when Tukārāma passed away, namely 1650 A.D. (Śake 1572), when Rāmadāsa came to settle on the banks of the Kṛishṇā, namely 1634 A.D. (Śake 1556), and when Śivājī captured the Toraṇā Fort, namely 1649 A.D. (Śake 1571), thus bidding fair to become the king of Mahārāshṭra later on, it is not impossible that Tukārāma might have met both Rāmadāsa and Śivājī. If the tradition were merely a tradition unsupported by any documentry evidence, we would have consented to allow the meeting to be regarded as well-nigh legendary. But we have certain Abhaṅgas which are supposed to have been composed by Tukārāma for the sake of Śivājī, which will not allow us to regard the meeting as entirely unhistorical. Tukārāma performed his Kīrtanas at Dehū, as well as at Lohagaon. Now Poona is situated just between Dehū and Lohagaon, and Śivājī had already a lodgment at Poona. Hence, it is not impossible that Śivājī might have gone to Tukārāma, seen him, and expressed a desire to be initiated by him. But, Tukārāma with foresight probably sent

Śivājī to Rāmadāsa. Some of the Abhaṅgas of Tukārāma addressed to Śivājī have been translated in the next chapter. Here, we may just give a glimpse of how Tukārāma once expatiated upon the theme of heroism, both worldly and spiritual, which was also, in all probability, meant for Śivājī. The Abhaṅgas are known as पाइकीचे अभंग, Abhaṅgas of soldiery or heroism. Tukārāma tells us that a hero is a hero both in worldly as well as in spiritual matters. "Without heroism, misery cannot disappear. Soldiers must become reckless of their lives, and then God takes up their burden. . . . He who bravely faces volleys of arrows and shots and defends his master, can alone reap eternal happiness. . . . He alone, who is a soldier, knows a soldier, and has respect for him. They, who bear weapons only for the sake of bodily maintenance, are mere mercenaries. The true soldier alone stands the test of critical occasions." This Abhaṅga has been supposed to have been composed by Tukārāma with the object of comparing the worldly soldier with the spiritual soldier. Then, again, as regards Tukārāma having met Rāmadāsa at

Paṇḍharapūr, it is true that we have no documentary evidence, as we have in the case of Tukārāma and Śivājī. But we know very well how Rāmadāsa had established himself on the banks of the Kṛishṇā in 1644 A.D. (Śake 1566), that is to say, about six years before Tukārāma's death, and how Rāmadāsa once visited Paṇḍharapūr and composed a song telling us that God Viṭṭhala and Rāma were identical. It would be a strange thing if Tukārāma and Rāmadāsa, being the two greatest saints of Mahārāshṭra at the time, should not have met each other. The "story" is not entirely meaningless which tells us that Rāmadāsa and Tukārāma met at Paṇḍharapūr on the opposite banks of the river Bhīmā, the one weeping and the other bawling, and when their respective disciples asked them the meaning of these strange gestures, Tukārāma replied that he wept because people were so much merged in worldly matters that they would not know that the way out lay in the realisation of God; while Rāmadāsa said that he bawled out because in spite of his bawling out, people would not hear his spiritual cry. The story only serves to rule out the improbability of the two of the greatest saints of Śivājī's time not having met each other, and it would be an irony of fate if the tender-minded and the tough-minded saints had not met, and exchanged their thoughts with one another.

The Disciples of Tukārāma

6. Tukārāma had a distinguished galaxy of disciples, all absolutely devoted and full of admiration for him. Santājī Telī, who was one of the greatest disciples of Tukārāma, was a writer of Tukārāma's Abhaṅgas, along with Gaṅgārāma Mavāḷa, who was another. The MS. of Santājī Telī has been preserved to this day, and has been published by Mr. Bhāve. Rāmeśvarabhatta, whose ancestors were residents of the Karnātaka, had come and settled in the district of Poona, and he worshipped his tutelary deity, namely, the Vyāghreśvara at Vāgholī. He was given too much to priestly pride and ritualism, but was later converted from this barren life to a spiritualistic life by Tukārāma. Śivabā Kāsāra, who lived in

Lohagaon, first hated Tukārāma, but later became an ardent admirer of him. It was his wife, who, having been displeased with her husband for having become a disciple of Tukārāma, once poured hot water on the body of Tukārāma while he had once gone to Lohagaon. Mahādājīpant, the Kulkarni of Dehū, was a very honest and straightforward disciple of Tukārāma, who spent on the rebuilding of the temple of Viṭṭhala at Dehū every pie out of the extra proceeds of a farm which had been given to Tukārāma by his employer, but which he had refused to accept. Niḷobā, who was perhaps the greatest of Tukārāma's disciples, is said to have been initiated by Tukārāma in a dream in the year 1678 A.D. (Śake 1600). He lived at Pimpaḷaner, and continued the Vārkarī tradition of Tukārāma. Bahiṇābāī, whose Abhaṅgas have been recently discovered and printed, was a resident of Śiur, and had seen Tukārāma personally. Her account of Tukārāma's spiritual lineage has been already noticed by us as being of great historical value, and as Pāṅgārakar tells us, she later came under the influence of Rāmadāsa, who gave her an image of Māruti which is still worshipped in Bahiṇābāī's household. These constitute the greatest of the disciples of Tukārāma.

Editions of the Gāthās of Tukārāma

7. There are various collations called Gāthās of the Abhaṅgas of Tukārāma, of which we must quote here four of the most important. The exposition of Tukārāma's mystical career and teaching, given in the later chapters, follows closely the numbering of the Abhaṅgas in the edition of Vishṇubuvā Jog, who published his 1st edition of the Gāthā of Tukārāma in two volumes in 1909 A.D. (Śake 1831), which is in fact the first and the only attempt in Marāthi of presenting the original with a translation. Besides, Vishṇubuvā Jog spent his life in studying the Abhaṅgas of Tukārāma, and was well respected among the Vārkarīs at Paṇḍharapūr. He had an open mind, and was perhaps the greatest and the most enlightened among the Vārkarīs during the last quarter of the century. The second collection of Tukārāma's Abhaṅgas is the edi-

tion called the Induprakāsa edition, which was printed by the Government of Bombay with the help of Mr. S. P. Pandit in 1869 A.D. This is a very careful collation of the various recensions of Tukārāma's Gāthās based upon the MSS. at Dehū, Talegaon, Kaḍūsa and Paṇḍharapūr. Fraser and Marāthe's translation of Tukārāma's Gāthās follows this edition in point of numbering. A third edition is that of Mr. H. N. Apte, printed at the Aryabhushaṇa Press according to the MS. in the possession of the Baḍaves of Paṇḍharapūr. This is an edition which has got much traditional value, because the Vārkarīs perform their Bhajana according to the readings of that edition. Fourthly, Mr. Bhāve has recently published an edition of Tukārāma's "real Gāthā" as he calls it, which consists of thirteen-hundred Abhaṅgas according to the MS. of Santājī Jaganāḍe. There is no doubt that this is a very authentic collection, but it is also likely that it is not a complete collection. The other editions of Tukārāma's Abhaṅgas which have been printed will not interest our readers very much, and so we refrain from giving any account of them. Our order of exposition* follows, for the sake of the numbering of the Abhaṅgas, the edition of Vishṇubuvā Jog which we have above referred to, and which we heartily recommend to our readers for the sake of the Marāthi original and the translation.

---

* Recently, a Source-book of Tukārāma's Abhaṅgas has been published by us, which gives *seriatim* the Abhaṅgas referred to in our exposition of Tukārāma in the next two chapters.

CHAPTER 1

Tukārāma's Mystical Career

I. HISTORICAL EVENTS IN HIS LIFE

Introductory

1. A faithful account of Tukārāma's mystical development as traced through his Abhaṅgas is a subject hitherto unattempted, in the first place, because Tukārāma has left to us quite a large number of Abhaṅgas, and in the second place, because it is really a difficult thing to trace through his Abhaṅgas the order of his developing mystical experience. Yet an attempt has been made here to essay this difficult task with what success we leave our readers to judge. We shall try to present the account of Tukārāma's spiritual development in his own words, which will leave our readers free to form any conclusions they like in regard to the value of the data for the comparison of Tukārāma's spiritual experience with that of the great mystics of the West.

The Occasion of Tukārāma's Initiation

2. We shall begin by giving an account of Tukārāma's description of his own initiation. Tukārāma tells us that he was initiated by his spiritual teacher in a dream: "I imagined I met him while he was going to the river for a holy bath. He placed his hand upon my head, and asked me to give him some ghee for meals. Unfortunately, being in a dream, I could not give it to him. An obstacle having thus apparently arisen, my spiritual techer hastened away. He told me his spiritual lineage, namely, that it had come from Rāghava Chaitanya and Keśava Chaitanya. He told me also his own name which was Bābājī, and gave me the Mantra 'Rāma, Kṛishṇa, Hari' for meditation. As it was the 10th day of the bright half of Māgha, and as, moreover, it was a Thursday (a day sacred to the Guru), I accepted the mantra with the whole of my heart" (Abg. 3427). Now this Bābājī, who was the teacher of Tukārāma, has his Samādhi at Otūr, and one does not know whether Bābājī was actually living at the time of Tukārāma. In any case, Tukārāma tells us that he got his initiation in a dream, and with that his spiritual career began: "Verily, my teacher being cognisant of the aspirations of my heart bestowed upon me a Mantra I loved so well, and a Mantra also which was so easy to utter. Verily, there can be no difficulty in the uttering of that Mantra. By that Mantra, have many, who have gone from amongst us, crossed the ocean of life. To those who know, and to those who do not know, the Mantra has served as a raft to enable them to cross the ocean of life. Verily, I was put in possession of this raft—there is no limit to the grace of God Pāṇḍuraṅga!" (Abg. 3428).

Tukārāma's Family Lineage

3. Tukārāma was born of a poor family in the caste of the Kuṇabīs, that is to say, farmers. He feels glad that he was born a Kuṇabī; otherwise, he says, he would have died with arrogance. "Well done, O God! Tukārāma dances and touches Thy feet. Had I been a learned man, I would have brought calamities on me; would have scorned the service of the saints; . . . would have been subject to pride and arrogance would only have gone by the way by which other people have gone to the Hades. Greatness and arrogance would surely have brought me to hell" (Abg. 178). He tells us also that throughout his family lineage, he has been a Vārkarī of Paṇḍharī: "I have inherited this practice of going to a pilgrimage to Paṇḍharī from my ancestors. I recognise no other pilgrimage, and no other vow. My only vow is to make a fast on the Ekādaśī day, and to sing the name of God. I shall utter the name of God, which is verily what will last to the end of time" (Abg. 1599).

Tukārāma's Family Difficulties

4. As is often the case with the mystics, Tukārāma experienced every kind of difficulty in his life. "What shall I eat, and where shall I go? On whose support should I count and live in my village? The Patel of my village, as well as its other residents, have grown angry with me. Who will give me alms? People will say that I have lost touch with the world, and will drag me to the court. I have gone to the good people in my village, and have told them that these people are pursuing a poor man like myself. Verily, I am tired of the company of these people. I shall now go and find out Viṭṭhala" (Abg. 2995). Added to the forlornness in his village, Tukārāma experienced every difficulty within his family. His estate was all sold. Famine made havoc in his family. "By repentance, I am now remembering Thee. Life seems to me like vomit. Happy am I that my wife is a termagant. Happy am I that I have lost all reputation. Happy, that I have been disrespected by men. Happy, that I have lost all my cattle. Well it is that I have ceased to be ashamed among men. Well it is that I have come as a supplicant to Thee, O God! Well it is that I built a temple to Thee, and neglected by children and wife. . . . " (Abg. 3941). Tukārāma's wife was so much exasperated at the demeanour of Tukārāma, and particularly at the very kind way in which he treated his saintly guests, that she began to exclaim: "Why is it that people come to our house? Have they no business of their own? For the sake of God, my husband has entered into relationship with the whole world. Indeed, he is put to no trouble for speaking mere good words." "My wife," says Tukārāma, "does not like any of these things, and runs after my guests like a mad dog" (Abg. 3489). "Verily, saints have no business here," says the wife of Tukā, "they can get food without doing any work. Every man that meets me beats the Ṭāḷa, and creates a spiritual hubbub. These people are as good as dead, and have bade good-bye to shame. They do not look so much as to the means of maintaining themselves. Their wives cry in despair, and curse these people" (Abg. 3491). The whole array of calamities now befell Tukārāma. His father died, and he probably began to experience anxiety for his maintenance, as he had never done before. One of his wives died of starvation, and Tukā believed that she got absolution. His child died, and Tukā was glad that God deprived him of the cause of unreal affection. His mother died, and Tukā bade good-bye to all anxieties forever. These incidents only served to increase the love of Tukā for God. "Between us two," says Tukā to God, "nobody now intervenes to create an artificial barrier" (Abg. 394). All these things he took to be the indications of God's favour on him. "God shall never help His devotee to carry on his worldly existence in an easy manner, but would ward off every source of affection. If He were to make His devotee fortunate, that would serve merely to make him arrogant. Hence it is that God strikes His devotee with poverty. Were He to give him a good wife, his affections would be centred on her. Hence God endows His devotee with a termagant. Verily, I have personally experienced all these things," says Tukā. "Why need I speak about these matters to others?" (Abg. 2224).

Nāmadeva's Command to Tukārāma to Compose Poetry

5. While he was experiencing such difficulties, Tukā had on another occasion another dream, in which Nāmadeva, the saint of Paṇḍharapūr, who had lived about three hundred years before the age of Tukārāma, appeared before him, and ordered him to compose poetry. "Nāmadeva aroused me in my dream and came in the company of God. He told me that I should not mis-direct my words, but should give myself to composing poetry. He told me to measure poems, telling me that God was counting the measure. He patted me on the back, and made me conscious of my mission. He told me also that the numbers of Abhaṅgas to be composed was a hundred crores all told. What part of this number had been unattempted by Nāmadeva, Tukā made good by his own composition" (Abg. 3937). We know how Nāmadeva had taken a vow that he would compose altogether a hundred crores of Abhaṅgas. But as he entered Samādhi before that number was reached, he entrusted the mission of composing the rest to Tukārāma. The number seems fabulous but the meaning is that Tukā only carried on the mission of the spiritual elevation of Mahārāshṭra through literature, which Nāmadeva had set before him. Tukārāma felt glad that he saw God in a dream on account of Nāmadeva. "If thou allowest me, O God, I shall live in Thy company, or in the company of the Saints. I have left off a place, which otherwise I would have desired. Be not now indifferent to me, O God! How soever low my place, how soever mean my vocation, I shall take rest on Thy feet. I have verily seen Thee in a dream on account of Nāmadeva, and shall ever consider it a blessing upon me" (Abg. 3938). In this way,

Tukārāma was conscious of the great obligation which Nāmadeva had conferred upon him by bringing God along with him in his dream. It was also on account of this incident that Tukā was inspired to compose his lyrical poems. "I have composed poetry according to my light," says Tukā. "Whether it is good or bad, God only knows. For whom and on whose behoof these Abhaṅgas have been created, God alone knows, because they are His own handiwork. I, for myself, extricate myself from egoism, throw my entire burden upon God, and rest content" (Abg. 3385).

Tukārāma's Great Sorrow at his Poems Being Thrown into the River

6. When a number of poems had been composed, and when apparently Tukā was highly spoken of by the people of his village, he incurred the anger of those who were to all appearances more learned than he, and who therefore conspired to ruin the poetical reputation of Tukā. Once upon a time they caught hold of Tukārāma's poems, and threw them into the river Indrāyaṇī. Tukārāma felt extremely sorry at this sad turn which events had taken. He determined to try his luck, and invoked God to restore his poems to him, and in case this would not happen, he determined to commit suicide. "Why shall I compose poems any longer? Must I not be ashamed of doing so? Saints will verily laugh at me. Now has come the time when God must give the decision. Truth alone must prevail. Why should one undertake any work at all without having the backing of realisation? I can no longer maintain courage. A great ruffle has been produced in me" (Abg. 3505). Tukārāma thus determined to make a fast, until he received an assurance from God that his work was appreciated by Him. He continued his fasting penance for thirteen days, and did not partake of even a drop of water. "It is thirteen days, O God, that I have remained without food and drink. Thou art yet so unkind as not to give me any assurance even after this long period. Thou art hiding Thyself behind a stone image. Now, verily I shall commit suicide and hold Thee responsible for it; for long have I waited to receive an assurance; but in its absence, I shall now destroy my life" . . . (Abg. 1731). God could wait no longer and see the great agonies in which Tukā was merged. He made His appearance to him in the form of a youthful image, so Tukā tells us, and gave him comfort and assurance.

God's Appearance and Tukārāma's Thanksgiving

7. The Abhaṅgas which Tukārāma composed on that occasion have been left to us by Tukārāma himself, and we shall give them here in the very words in which Tukā has left them: "Thou, my God, who followest us poor men as the shadow the body, camest near me like a youth, and gavest comfort to me. You showed me your beautiful form, embraced me, and pacified my mind. . . . Verily have I troubled you for nothing. Forgive me, my God. I shall never cause you trouble any more" (Abg. 3522). "I committed a great fault, because I have taxed your patience. . . . Mean creature that I am, I shut my eyes and went on fasting for thirteen days. . . . You saved my books in the river, and protected me against the calumny of the people. Verily have you come to succour your devotee" (Abg. 3523). "Let people put a scythe against my neck, or give trouble to me as they please. I shall no longer do anything which will give you trouble. . . . Forgive me forwhat I have done before; I shall now guard myself against future events" (Abg. 3524). "What will you not do, O God, for the saints, if they keep patience? I grew impatient, and without intelligence as I was, I nevertheless received favour at your hands". . . (Abg. 3525). "Nobody had put a scythe on my neck, nor had anybody cudgelled me on my back, and yet I cried so much for your help. Compassionate as you were, you divided yourself in two places, near me and in the river, and saved both me and the books. . . . There is nobody who can be compared to you in point of compassion. Verily, my words fail to describe your greatness" (Abg. 3526). "You are more affectionate than a mother: You are more delightful than the moon. Your grace flows like a river. What comparison can I find for your qualities, O God? . . . You, who have made nectar, are really sweeter than it. . . . I place my head on Thy feet in silence. Forgive me, O God" (Abg.

3527) "I am a vicious and sinful man. Give me a place at Thy feet. Adieu to all to all worldly life which only moves the mind away from God's feet. The ripples of intellect change from moment to moment, and attachment ends in dislodging us from fixity of any kind. Put an end to all my anxieties, O God, and come to live in my heart" (Abg. 3528).

Tukārāma and Rāmeśvarbhatta

8. Tukārāma continued to be persecuted by the evil men in his native place, and Rāmeśvarbhatta, a learned Brahmin who did not know what spiritual life was, was probably one of the greatest of the persecutors of Tukārāma. Once upon a time, it is reported, some bad men threw boiling water on the body of Tukārāma as he was passing by. That put Tukārāma in a state of agony. "My body is burning; I feel as if I am actually burning in fire," says Tukārāma. "Run to my help, O God. My very hairs are aflame. The body is cremated unto death. It is bursting into two parts. Why do you wait any longer, O God? Run to my succour with water. Nobody else can help me. You are

verily my Mother, who can save her devotee at the time of distress" (Abg. 3956). And as Nemesis would have it, Rāmeśvarbhatta himself, who was the cause of the above suffering, himself suffered great bodily distress on another occasion, and failing every resource to cure it, was ultimately obliged to go to Tukārāma for succour. Tukārāma, magnanimous as he was, composed an Abhaṅga for him, by which, it is said, Rāmeśvarbhatta was relieved from his suffering: "If the mind is pure, then verily even enemies become friends; neither tigers nor serpents can hurt them in any way; poison may become nectar; a blow may become a help; what ought not to be done may itself open for him the path of moral action; sorrow will be the cause of happiness; and the flames of fire will become cool; all these things will happen when one knows that there is the same immanent Being in the hearts of all" (Abg. 3957).

Rāmeśvarbhatta's Description of His Own Conversion

9. Rāmeśvarbhatta tells us the way in which, after a life of hatred towards Tukārāma, he began to conceive a respect for him, and ultimately became his disciple. "As a result of my hatred towards Tukārāma," Rāmeśvarbhatta tells us, "I suffered great bodily anguish. Jñāneśvara appeared to me in a dream, and told me that I had contracted the disease, as I had censured Tukārāma who was the incarnation of Nāmadeva, and the greatest of all Saints. Jñāneśvara also told me to be submissive towards Tukārāma, and in that way, there would be an end to my sin. Believing in the dream, I made up my mind to attend his Kīrtana every day. It was in Tukārāma's company that my body became whole" (Abg. 4145). "However learned a man may be, and however well-versed in the Vedas, he can never equal Tukārāma. Neither those who read the Purāṇas, nor those who study the Bhagavadgītā, can come to know the secret of spiritual life. The Brāhmaṇas in this bad age have been spoilt by their arrogance about caste, and by the consciousness of their superiority. Tukārāma was a Bania after all, and yet he loved God, and therefore his words were as sweet as nectar. Tukārāma merely expounded the real meaning of the Vedas. . . . By his devotion, his knowledge, and his dispassionateness, he was without equal. . . . Many great Saints have lived in times of old, but it is only Tukā who took his body to heaven. Rāmeśvarbhatta says that Tukā took leave of all men, and went to heaven in a Vimāna" (Abg. 4144).

A Piece of Tukārāma's Autobiography

10. Tukārāma had by this time become fixed in God. As he had put his faith in the Name which his preceptor had imparted to him, meditated on it, and made it the stepping stone to God-realisation, he was able to say that he had crossed the ocean of life. In two or three different places, Tukārāma tells us how it was the name which had saved him through life. He gives us a piece of autobiography, which we narrate here in his own words: "Salutation to God, and salutation to the Saints. . . . Tukā is verily the servant of his teacher Bābājī. How will my words be able to please the Saints? I will at least try to please my own mind. Let my mind go after the name of God, and sing His praises. My early life was embittered by calamities; but the Name gave me comfort. The happiness I derived by meditation on the Name was incomparable. The Impersonal took on a form. I found that God runs to the place where the Name is celebrated. Make haste to sing the praise of God. Everything else leads to sorrow. . . . From those who disbelieve in the Name, God stands at a distance. . . . The Name is verily the pathway to heaven. . . . Those who have known tell us to meditate on the Name by leaving away all arrogance. . . . Those, who know and those who do not know, to them I say, meditate on the Name. In this way will you be saved. I have personally known how a sinner could be saved. There could be no greater sinner than myself: other people may have stored some merit at least. To me there was no other pathway except the Kīrtana. I found that the saint need not be afraid of his sustenance: God will find ways and means for him. God will follow the Saint, look at his feet, and cleanse his path by his robe. . . . God has really saved me. There is no limit to the kindness of God" (Abg. 3935, 1-23). "Verily, I am a great sinner," says Tukā in another place, "I wonder why I should be the object of your love, O Saints! I know in my innermost heart that I have not attained the goal of my life. But people say that I have attained it, and follow one another in saying so. I was greatly worried in my life. I tended the cattle, but that was not enough for my maintenance. What money I had, I spent on myself and did not give in charity to Brahmins and sages. I got wearied of my relatives, wife, children, and brothers. . . . I could not show my face to the people. Then I began to take recourse to the woods. Hence it was that I began to like solitude. I was greatly worried on account of family expenses, and I became very unkind. My ancestors worshipped this God, and I have inherited that worship from them. Do not suppose that I have got any high-strung devotion" (Abg. 3940). Yet, in another place, Tukārāma tells us at greater length and with more personal touches the story of his own conversion. "I was born a Śūdra, and was doing the duty which had fallen to my lot by the rules of caste. This deity Viṭṭhala has been worshipped throughout the history of my family. I should not have said anything about my personal life; but because you

Saints have asked me about it, I say a few words. I was merged in much sorrow in my worldly life. My mother and father died. My wealth was all spent in a famine. I was dishonoured. My wife died, because there was no food to eat. I was ashamed, and got disgusted with my life. My trade became meagre. The temple which I wished to build fell to the ground. Originally, I fasted on the Ekādaśī day and performed a Kīrtana. My mind was not set on devotional practices originally. In full faith, and with full respect, I learnt by heart some sayings of the bygone Saints. With pure heart and devotion, I sang after the men who performed the Kīrtana. I tasted of the water on the feet of the saints; nor did I allow any shame to creep into my mind. I conferred obligations upon others as far as lay in my power, not minding any bodily hardships. I took no account of what my friends said about me. I became entirely disgusted about my life. . . . I never cared for the opinion of the majority. I relied only upon the instruction of my Teacher in the dream, and believed fully in the power of Name. Then, I was encouraged to compose poetry, which I did with full faith in God Viṭṭhala. I was, however, obliged to drown my poems in the river, which greatly upset my mind. I sat fasting at the door of God, and He ultimately comforted me. The many incidents of my life will take me long to describe. I may say that I am content with what has happened. What is to happen further, God only knows. I know only this that God shall never neglect His Saint. I know how kind He has been to me. This is the treasure of my life, which God Viṭṭhala has made me give out" (Abg. 3939).

Some Miracles of Tukārāma

11. As a saint grows old, miracles inevitably gather round about him. Even so did it happen in the case of Tukārāma. Once upon a time, while he was engaged in performing a Kīrtana at Lohagaon, a woman brought her dead child, threw it before Tukā, and charged him that if he were a real Saint, he would raise that child; upon which, it has been related, that Tukārāma raised the child. There is an Abhaṅga of Tukārāma probably referring to this incident: "It is not impossible for Thee, O God, to bring to life a dead being. Have we not heard of Thy prowess in history? Why shouldst Thou not do a similar act at present? Fortunate are we that we call ourselves the servants of God. Pour a balm on my eyes," says Tukā, "by showing the greatness of Thy power" (Abg. 3955). On one occasion, while Tukārāma was engaged in a Kīrtana and Śivājī was attending it, the enemies of Śivājī surrounded the place where the Kīrtana was going on, upon which, there was a hue and cry among the people that had assembled for Kīrtana; and, it has been related, that as Tukā began to implore God to ward off the danger, God appeared in the form of Śivājī, and tried to escape from the hands of the enemies. Whereupon, the enemies pursued him, leaving Tukārāma and the real Śivājī unmolested at the place of the Kīrtana. Tukārāma's Abhaṅga in this connection runs as follows: "How would it be possible for me to see this great disaster with my eyes? My heart is filled with sorrow to see others in calamity. Thou must not see the disaster happen to us! We have never heard that where the servants of God dwell, the enemies can come and molest them. Tukā says, my devotion has been put to shame. I shall be living only as a contemptible being in the eyes of others" (Abg. 3951). "I am not afraid of death. But I cannot see other people plunged in misery. . . . That one's mind should be upset at the time of Kīrtana is itself a kind of death. Give me, O God, says Tukā, shelter at a place where there is no danger" (Abg. 3952). "Shall I believe what has been said about the Kīrtana of God, that where it is begin celebrated, people are relieved of their miseries? On the other hand, there is here a great danger: the enemies have almost laid a siege. I have come to know in person that without sin no sin can take place. How shall I now believe that Thou residest where Thy servants live?" (Abg. 3953), upon which, it is said, that the enemies were put on a false scent by God, and Śivājī and Tukārāma escaped the danger. The meeting of Tukārāma and Śivājī does not seem to be unhistorical, and we must remember the famous verse which Tukārāma sent to Śivājī, in which he said that the ant and the king were to him alike. "My delusion and desires are at an end. They are verily the bait which death sets for us. Gold and clay are to me of equal consequence. The whole heaven has descended into my house" says Tukā (Abg. 3391); so saying, it has been said, that Tukārāma refused to accept the treasure which Śivājī had sent him.

Tukārāma and Jñāneśvara

12. Once upon a time it so happened that a Brahmin went to the temple of Jñāneśvara at Āḷandī, and sat there in meditation with a desire that he might receive some spiritual illumination from him. After some days, the Brahmin dreamt a dream, in which he was advised by Jñāneśvara to go to Tukārāma, who was living at that time. The Brahmin came to Tukārāma and told him what had happened in the dream; whereupon Tukārāma composed eleven Abhaṅgas, the substance of which is as follows: "Do not follow the lore of the learned books. Take a vow that you would seek the grace of God by emptying your heart of its innate desires. . . . God will come to your rescue by the power of the Name, and take you across the ocean of life" (Abg. 3363). "God does not possess salvation ready-made, so that He may hand it over to His devotee. Salvation consists in conquering the senses and mind, and making them empty of the pursuit of objects".... (Abg. 3364) . . . "Invoke the grace of God, asking his compassion on you, and make your mind your onlooker.... Tukā says that God is an ocean of compassion, and will relieve you of the thraldom of existence in a moment's time" (Abg. 3365). "If you meditate on the name of Govinda, then you will become Govinda yourself. There will be no difference between you and God. The mind will be filled with joy, and the eyes will shed down tears of love".... (Abg. 3366). "Why do you become small? You are really as large as the universe itself. Take leave of your worldly life, and make haste. Because you think yourself a small being, therefore you are merged in darkness, and are grieved" (Abg. 3370). . . . "The king of learned men, and their spiritual teacher, you are worthily called Jñānadeva. Why should such a low man as myself be made great? A shoe on the foot must be placed only on the foot. Even gods themselves cannot be compared to you. How would then other people be compared to you? But I do not know your purpose, and hence I humbly bend my head before you" (Abg. 3372). "A child speaks any words it pleases. It behooves you, great Saint, to excuse its lisping. I have taken no account of my station. Keep me near your feet, O Jñāneśvara," implores Tukā (Abg. 3373).

The Final Scene of Tukārāma's Life

13. Tukārāma had now reached the summit of his spiritual power. His fame as a Saint had spread far and wide. From the life of an ordinary Kunabī, he had risen to be the Spiritual King of the world. By performing Kīrtanas, and by spreading the glory of God's Name, he had been the cause of conferring infinite obligation on his devotees. He enjoyed every spiritual bliss in the world, and was waiting only for the final scene. When the time arrived, he tells us, God came in person to take him to heaven. "See, God comes there with the conch and the disc in His hands. The eagle, His favourite messenger, comes with ruffled pinions, and says to me 'fear not, fear not.' By the lustre of the crown of the gems on God's head, even the Sun fades into insignificance, God has a form blue like the sky, and is infinitely handsome. He has four hands, and down His neck hangs the garland called Vaijayantī. By the lustre of His lower clothes, the quarters are filled with light. Tukā is filled with gladness that the very heaven has descended into his house" (Abg. 3606). And when God Himself came to invite him, Tukārāma did not think it proper to live any longer in the world. He bade good-bye to the people. "I go to heaven. Compassion be on me from all of you," says Tukā. "Tender my supplications to all. God Pāṇḍuraṅga is standing up for a long time, and is calling me to heaven. At the last moment of my life, God has come to take me away, and Tukā disappears with his body" (Abg. 3616). As to whether Tukārāma did actually take his body to heaven, we have no other evidence from him to determine except this Abhaṅga, and the only meaning that we can make out of it is that his very physical existence had become divine as the time had come for him to ascend to Heaven.

II. TUKĀRĀMA AS A SPIRITUAL ASPIRANT

Introductory

14. We have hitherto considered the incidents in Tukārāma's life as we gather them authentically from his works. Starting from the life of a Kuṇabī, we see how ultimately he merged in God. But though we have considered merely Tukārāma's external life-history hitherto, we have not taken any account of the history of his soul: how he commenced his spiritual life, what difficulties he met with on the way, what heart-rendings he had to experience in his lone journey, how ultimately a gleam of light began to shine on him, until finally how he realised God and became one with Him. The history of Tukārāma's soul, therefore, will occupy our attention for the three sections to come. In the first, we shall consider Tukārāma as a spiritual aspirant. Then, we shall go to consider the heart-rendings of Tukārāma when he was unable to find God. Finally, we shall consider how Tukārāma was able to realise God, and enter into union with Him. There is a sort of a Hegelian dialectic in Tukārāma's soul. In the first stage of his spiritual career, he seems to have resolved to withdraw himself from the life of the world with a determined effort to win spiritual knowledge. This is the stage of positive affirmation. Then comes the stage of negation, the dark night of Tukārāma's soul, a stage where Tukārāma is warring with his own self. Finally, there is the stage of a new affirmation, namely, the cancellation of the original determination and the middle negation into a final vision of the God-head, which supersedes them both. We shall first see how Tukārāma weaned his mind from the world with a determination to achieve his spiritual purpose.

Tukārāma Bids Good-bye to the Manners of the World

15. Tukārāma begans his spiritual career by girding up his loins against the life of sin " . . . I have now determined to achieve the end. I shall never part with the treasure in my possession. Adieu now to all idleness which is the canker of the soul. Adieu to all forgetfulness which prevents one from harbouring God in his mind. Adieu to all shame, for it stands in the way of the attainment of God. Happy am I, that I have determined to find out God" (Abg. 2774). He imposes upon his mind an extreme severity in social relations. "How long shall I tell my mind not to run after everybody it sees? Idle affection is the cause of sorrow. Real happiness consists in leading a severe social life. Care not for praise or blame. Care not for compassion and affection. Care not for happiness and sorrow. Do not those who want to pursue God sit down at a place with a determined effort to find out God? Think about it, my mind," says Tukā, "and be as hard as adamant" (Abg. 594). He expresses this same attitude elsewhere when he tells us that he had grown entirely indifferent to the amenities of social life. "Speak not with me" says Tukā. "Let people be as they are. My only business with them is to bid them goodbye as soon as I see them. Who can ever find time to mix with others? These people are merged in all sorts of fantastic activities. At a stroke," says Tukā, "I have come out of the manners of the world" (Abg. 1514).

Tukārāma Invites Deliberate Suffering

16. Tukārāma even craves deliberate misery in order that it might lead him to God. "Make me homeless, wealthless, childless" says Tukā, "so that I may remember Thee. Give no child to me, for by its affection, Thou shalt be away from me. Give me not either wealth or fortune, for, that is a calamity itself. Make me a wanderer," says Tukā, "for, in that way alone I may be able to remember Thee night and day" (Abg. 2084). He elsewhere says also: "Let me get no food to eat, nor any child to continue my family line; but let God have mercy on me. This is what my mind tells me, and I keep telling the same thing to the people. Let my body suffer all sorts of calumnies, or adversities; but let God live in my mind. All these things verily are perishable," says Tukā; "for God alone is happiness" (Abg. 247).

The Evanescence of the Human Body

17. "What use is there of this mortal body?" asks Tukā. "To feed on dainties and dishes is the life's ideal for the ignorant. People say that we should protect the body; but of what use is that? They do not know that ours is a perishable existence, and we will go out all of a sudden. Death will come and eat up our body like a ball of food. People have deliberately thrust scimitars in their bodies, have cut off pieces of their flesh, and like Śuka have betaken themselves to the forest. Did not king Janaka," asks Tukā, "rule over his kingdom at the same time that he was placing one of his feet in the fire"? (Abg. 248). All this is as much as to say that as a spiritual aspirant, Tukārāma advises us to cease to take care of the body. He discants upon the infirmities of old age. "Old age comes and tells a tale in the ear that Death will soon pounce on the body. Why should not the mind grow alert at such a message? . . . In no time shall the last scene take place. . . . Think of the family deity," says Tukā, "and leave away empty words" (Abg. 1914). Tukārāma tells people to put themselves in mind of Death when they see the cremation of others. Tukārāma probably whetted his own mind to spirituality at the sight of the cremation of others by fire. "You see the burning of other people's bodies. Why does it not make you alert? Cry after God without fear, before death has caught hold of you. Death is verily a price which the body has to pay. . . . Why do people vainly seek after various paths? When death comes upon you, it shall not allow you to move even an inch" (Abg. 1006). In another place, Tukārāma asks: "Why do not people keep themselves awake when the robber is committing a theft in the neighbour's house? Why do you merge yourselves in forgetfulness? Your intellect has taken leave of you. Thieves are robbing everything that you possess, and are putting up a false appearance before you. You are entertaining a false idea. You never care to protect your inmost treasure: at least try to protect it now," says Tukā (Abg. 1106).

Nobody Can Rescue One From the Clutches of Death Except God Himself

18. "It seems wonderful," says Tukā, "that people should rely upon anything except God to rescue them from the clutches of death. It is strange that people should not take thought of what would ultimately conduce to their benefit. Upon what do these people rely? Who can help them at the final end? What can they say to the messengers of Death? Have they forgotten Death? Upon what treasure do these people count? . . . Why do not they remember God in order to get away from the bondage of life? . . ." (Abg. 943). "People love you because you give money to them. But nobody would help you at the time of death. When your bodily power has gone, when your eyes and nose are sending down excreta, your children and wife will leave you in the lurch, and run away. Your wife will say, 'much better that this ass should die: he has spoilt the whole house by his spits.' Tukārāma says that nobody else can come to your rescue except God" (Abg. 2178). "Do not get yourself entangled," says Tukā, "in the meshes of worldly life; for death is approaching you to make a morsel of you. When he pounces upon you, neither your mother nor your father can rescue you; neither the king, nor the governor of your place; neither your relatives, howsoever good." Tukā says that nobody can rescue you out of the clutches of death except God Himself (Abg. 2035).

The Spiritual Value of Mortal Existence

19. It was probably with a continual contemplation of the power of death that Tukārāma fortified his mind against any impending bodily calamities. But we must not say that he was not conscious of the great merit that belonged to the body if used well. "The body is verily a wish-jewel," he tells us. "It will yield you all desires if you put an end to all egosim, and if you make your mind as clear as a crystal by leaving away all censure, injury, and deceit. Such a man need not go to a place of pilgrimage to get absolution. He will himself be a place of pilgrimage, and people will flock to him and get absolution at his sight. When the mind is pure, what is the use of those garlands and those ornaments? The Saint will himself be an ornament to all ornaments. He always utters the name of God, and his mind is ever full of joy. He has given over his body and mind and wealth to God, and is entirely without desire. Such a man is greater than a touch-stone and is impossible to describe" (Abg. 28). From this, we see that, provided the body is used well, it may itself be an instrument for the revelation of

God. "Even gods desire this mortal existence" says Tukā. "Blessed are we that we were ever born, and have become the servants of God. By means of this life, and in this very life, we can attain to the Godhead. We can make heaven the stepping-stone to divine existence" (Abg. 119).

Tukārāma Binds God With Love

20. Tukārāma seems to have determined to turn his mortal existence to the best account possible. He prays to God to allow his mind to rest on His feet wherever his body may be. "This is my prayer to Thee, O God. I place my head on Thy feet. Let my body be where it likes, but let my mind always rest on Thy feet. Let me spend my time in meditating on Thee. Let me turn away from body, and mind, and wealth. Release me at the time of death from such dangers as phlegm, and wind, and bile. So long as my senses are whole, I have called upon Thee, in order that Thou mightest help me ultimately" (Abg. 2430). In the midst of his life's duties, Tukārāma's one interest was to remember the feet of God. "I do the duty which has fallen to me, but I always remember Thy feet. Why should I give expression to my love? Thou knowest it already. I look at Thy form at all times, and somehow carry on my worldly existence. I have appointed my speech to sing Thy praise. My mind is anxious to have a vision of Thee without any craving for money or wealth. I am walking my worldly way, as a man must who has a burden to carry; but my mind is ever set on Thee. . . . " (Abg. 2050). He says to God that he would never be afraid of Him, provided he can continue to have devotion for him. "To find out God, I know a remedy. We need not be afraid of God. What power can He have? We should pray to Him in all humility, and then, we will be able to find Him. He will then do whatever He likes. Merely by the power of devotion, we may be able to attain to Him. Thus will I bind God by the cords of my love". . . . (Abg. 543). The same idea Tukārāma reiterates in another passage when he says that wherever God may go, He will find spread for Him the omnipresent meshes of Tukārāma's love. "Wherever Thou mayest go, Thou shalt see me. Thus, far and wide shall I spread my love. There will be no place which Thou canst then call Thine own. My mind, which is set on Thee, will watch Thee everywhere. . . . " (Abg. 1064). Tukārāma also employs one or two metaphors to describe the manner in which to love God. He tells us in one place that he will enclose God within him, as a tortoise encloses its feet. "Thy secret I have come to know by the power of my devotion. I have enclosed Thy form within me, as a tortoise encloses its feet. I shall never allow Thy form to melt away" (Abg. 182). Again, Tukārāma says that he will be a bird on the creeper of God's Name. "The creeper of God's Name has spread far and wide, and has attained to flower and fruit. On it my mind will be a royal bird and eat to its satisfaction. The seed has shown its sweetness. Why should I not catch hold of the fruit? As one allows time to pass by, one will surely miss the sweetness of the fruit" (Abg. 2401).

Tukārāma Pants for the Company of the Saints

21. The most important help, however, for the realisation of God is the company of the Saints, and Tukārāma expresses an earnest desire for the company of those who love God. "Let me meet people of my own kind, so that I may be satisfied. My mind pants to meet those who love God. My eyes keep a watch to see them. My life will be blessed only when I go and embrace those Saints. Only on that day shall I be able to sing God to my satisfaction" (Abg. 1316). It was with that view that Tukārāma prayed to God not to make him dependent on false prophets. "As I go to see God in the houses of the learned, I find only arrogance in those places. When I go to see those who recite the Vedas, I see that they only quarrel with one another. When I go to seek Self-knowledge, I find quite its opposite in those places. Those who have no control over their mind growl with anger, and falsely call themselves Gurus. Make me not dependent, O God, upon such false prophets" (Abg. 980). "I have left off everything and clung to Thy feet. I would much rather be the sands and pebbles in Paṇḍharapūr. I shall touch the feet of the Saints who go to Paṇḍharī. I shall even be the shoes and slippers on the feet of such Saints. I would not mind being even a cat or a dog in the possession of these Saints. I would even be a well or a stream, so that the Saints might come and wash their feet in it. If I am to be of any service to the Saints, I shall not be afraid of rebirth" (Abg. 3141). It was this spirit of Tukārāma which made the Saints reciprocate the feelings of Tukā. Tukārāma's obligations to the Saints knew no bounds. "How shall I express my obligations to the Saints? They keep me ever awake. How shall I be able to repay their kindness? If I sacrifice my life at their feet, that would be insufficient. They speak unconsciously, and yet impart great spiritual knowledge. They come to me, and love me, as the cow does the calf" (Abg. 2787). Thus in every way Tukārāma kept himself alert. He watched himself every moment, and became his own on-looker. He tenaciously clung to the feet of God. He became awake as he had previously experienced the fear of life's misery (Abg. 827).

III. THE DARK NIGHT OF TUKĀRĀMA'S SOUL

"I Have Not Seen Thee Even in My Dreams."

22. But not with all his determination to achieve the spiritual end would Tukā be so fortunate as to win God at once. The attainment of God involves infinite trouble and a perpetual racking of the soul. To the positive determination of the spiritual aspirant comes to be contrasted the negative psychology of the man who is in the throes of God-realisation. It was thus with Tukārāma. Not with all his efforts to know God would Tukārāma find that it was easy for him to reach God. "My heart tells me," he says "that I have not known Thee. A tin-plate cannot have the colour of brass. The child of a concubine cannot know its father. People will come to know that I am not as they have supposed me to be" (Abg. 1475). He tells us in another passage that it would be impossible for him to dance with joy, unless he has known God. "I have come to know the intentions of God," he says. "He deceives me and makes me serve, without bestowing His knowledge upon me. . . . But He does not know that I am a Bania after all, and that I cannot be so easily cheated. How can I dance with joy unless I have known God?" (Abg. 1257). Tukārāma confesses that he has not seen God even in dreams. "How am I not able to see Thy beautiful form even in dreams? I have not seen Thy four-handed vision, with a garland coming down Thy neck, and with a beautiful mark of Kasturi on Thy forehead. . . . Show me Thy form at least in my dream, O God," says Tukā (Abg. 3257). He tells us furthermore that his desires have remained unfulfilled. He feels forlorn for not having had a fantasy of God even in his dream. "What I demanded of Thee has been of no avail. My trouble has remained. Thou hast never given comfort to me, nor fulfilled my wishes. I have not had even a fantasy of Thee even in my dreams. . . . I feel ashamed of sitting in the company of the Saints. I have lost all courage. I think I am forlorn" (Abg. 2505).

Tukārāma's Desire to See the Four-handed Vision

23. Tukārāma sets up as the ideal of his early spiritual life the vision of the four-handed Person, namely, God. He would be satisfied with nothing but that vision. "Honour among men, happiness of the body, all kinds of prosperity are merely a tantalising of the soul. Therefore come to me, O God. . . . What shall I do with mere argumentative knowledge about You? . . . It is merely a secondary consideration. Nothing can satisfy me except the vision of the four-handed God. . . . My Soul likes nothing but Your own vision, and pines for the realisation of Your feet" (Abg. 1161). "How shall I be able to know Thy intimate nature? The Sciences proclaim that there is no limit to Thy form. Take Thou on a spiritual form for me, and show me Thy four-handed vision. It would not be possible for me—a mortal being—to see Thy infinite form, which is above the heavens and below the nether worlds. I fully believe, O God, that Thou takest on a form according to the desire of Thy devotee" (Abg. 1719). "And I wish to see the same form which You have shown to bygone saints, Uddhava, Akrūra, Vyāsa, Ambaṛishi, Rukmāṅgada and Prahlāda. I am keenly desirous to see Thy beautiful face and feet. I am desirous to know in what shape You appeared in the house of Janaka, and how You ate the poor food of Vidura; how You favoured the Pāṇḍavas in the midst of danger; how You saved Draupadī when her honour was being lost;

how You played with the Gopīs; how You gave happiness to the cows and the cowherd boys. Show me that form of Yours, so that my eyes may remain satisfied" (Abg. 1163). "Former saints have described Thee. How, by the force of their devotion, Thou hast taken on a small form! Show me Thy small form, O God. Having seen Thee, I shall speak with Thee. I shall embrace Thy feet, shall set my eyes on them, and shall stand before Thee with my hands folded together. This is my innermost desire, which nobody else except Thee can satisfy" (Abg. 716).

Extreme Restlessness of Tukārāma's Mind

24. "I have become mad after Thee, O God. I am vainly looking in the various directions for Thee. I have left off all Samsāra and the worldly manners. My eyes pine after seeing Thy form, of which my ears have heard. The very foundations of my life are shaken, and I pant without Thee as a fish without water" (Abg. 2210). "Are You engaged elsewhere to attend to a devotee's call? Or, are You fallen asleep?

You may have been caught in the meshes of the Gopis' devotion, and may be looking at their faces! Are You engaged in warding off some dangers of Your devotees? Or, is the way far off, that You have to cross? Do You see my faults that You do not come? Tell me the reason, O God. My life is really oozing out of my eyes," says Tukā (Abg. 1019). "My mind is fixed on Thee, as a beggar's mind is fixed on rich food. My heart is set on Thy feet, and my life-principle is dwindling. As a cat sits looking at a ball of butter ready to pounce upon it, so do I sit waiting for Thee, my Mother" (Abg. 3018). "As verily a young girl, who is going to her father-in-law's house, wistfully casts her glance at her home, similarly do I look at Thee and wish to know when I shall meet Thee. As a child that misses its mother, or as a fish that comes out of water, similarly do I pant after Thee," says Tukā (Abg. 131). "Shall I ever be fortunate to enjoy Thee without a moment's respite? When, O when, shall I enjoy that mental state? Shall I ever be so fortunate as to reap the divine bliss? Will ever God be pleased to give it to me?" (Abg. 2377). "I ask everybody I meet, will God help me? Will

God have compassion on me, and save me from shame? Verily, I have forgotten everybody, and my only business is to think about God. Shall I ever be fortunate to see one who will be able to tell me when I may meet God?" (Abg. 689). "Shall I ever be able to reach Thee like the Saints of old? When I think how the Saints of old have known Thee, I suffer from extreme restlessness. I am a bondsman of my senses. They, on the other hand, were filled with happiness. I cannot curb a single sense. How shall I be able to curb them all? If Thou leavest me at this stage, I shall be as good as nought" (Abg. 319).

Tukārāma's Constant Warfare With the World and the Mind

25. Added to his extreme desire to see God and his inability to find Him, was the continual internal and external warfare which Tukā was carrying on in his life. "I am always warring," he says, "with the world and with the mind. Accidents befall me all of a sudden, and I try to ward them off by the power of Thy name" (Abg. 3140). "Yet, I am afraid on account of the darkness of the journey. All the quarters to me have become lone and dreadful, and I do not find anybody worth loving. I see herds of dangerous beasts and I lose all courage. The darkness prevents my journey, and I fall at every stump and stem. Alone, without a second, I find numerous paths opening out before me, and I am afraid to take to any one of them. My Guru has shown me the way no doubt, but God is yet far away" (Abg. 2504). As Tukā found desolation in the external world, so he found it also in the internal world. "Save me, O God," he says, "from the wanderings of my mind. It is always agile, and never rests for a moment. Be not now indifferent to me, O God. Run to the succour of this poor soul. Run before my various senses have torn off my mind into pieces. All my personal endeavour has been at an end: I am only waiting to have Thy grace" (Abg. 1136).

Tukārāma's Consciousness of His Faults

26. Tukārāma became at this stage keenly conscious of his own defects, as happens with all progressive mystics, and an introspective analysis of his mind put him in torments of self-calumny. Time and oft, Tukārāma calls in the help of God to save him from his faults. Any personal effort to remove the signs of sins and faults became insufficient, and an external help was invoked for the purification of his mind. "I know my own faults too well, O God. But I cannot help the wanderings of my mind. Now stand between myself and my mind, and show Thy compassion. . . . I have solely become a slave to my senses. Be not indifferent to me, O God, however wicked I may be" (Abg. 2082). "My mind tells me that my conduct is wicked. I know my faults too well. Thou knowest everything, O God, and mayest do as Thou pleasest. I have now fallen on Thy compassion. Thou mayest do whatever Thou thinkest fit" (Abg. 1902). "I even think of the merits which I once possessed. I now feel I have lost all of them. My mind tells me that my capital has been lost. I think about the faults of others in order to make myself an object of praise. I have become like a cock which pecks ahead, and which while pecking loses its food" (Abg. 1454). "I have been verily ashamed of the spiritual life. I do not think that Thou mayest accept me. My mind does not stand still. It turns from object to object. I have been enchained by pseudo-greatness, and have given over my neck to be tied by the cords of affection. My body wishes to partake of dainties to which it is accustomed, and I do not like bad things. I have been a mine of faults," says Tukā; "my idleness and sleep know no bounds" (Abg. 2780). "I have assumed a saintly exterior, but have not bidden good-bye to the things of the world. I recall to mind this fact every day. . . . My mind has not come out of the worldly life, and is persistently doing the same things over and over again. I have become like a Bahurūpi, and am never internally as I seem to be" (Abg. 465).

Tukārāma's Description of His Own Vices

27. Tukārāma even goes to consider how his life has been a perpetual scene of vice and misery. "Cursed be my egoism. Cursed be my fame. There is no limit to my sin and to my misery. I have become a burden to this earth. How much have I suffered? My sorrow would break a hard stone. Men do not even so much as look at me. In body, speech, and mind, I have done evil things. My eyes, hands and feet have been the slaves of sin. Censure, hatred, betrayal, adultery: how much should I narrate my own defects? By the consciousness of my little wealth, I became arrogant. My house was rent on account of my having two wives. I have disrespected my father's words. I have been a thoughtless, crooked, duty-avoiding, censurable wrangler. How many more of my defects shall I enumerate? My speech is unable to mention them. My mind trembles to think of them. I showed no compassion to the poor, conferred no obligations on them, had no courage of words, have been entirely addicted to sex: I cannot even mention these things in words. Hear, O Saints, how my vices and thoughtlessness have increased my sin! Make me acceptable to God, O Saints! I have come in submission before you" (Abg. 2062). In another place, he tells us the same story: "Masterless as I was, I have been the source of many faults. No dutiful action has relieved my conduct.

I have been a man of dull apprehension. I have never remembered Thee, O compassionate Lord! I have never heard or sung Thy prayer. I have entertained false shame. I have not known the way to realisation. I have never heard the Saints' stories. On the other hand, I have much reproached and censured the Saints. I have never conferred any obligations on others. I have shown no compassion in teasing others. I have done things which I should never have done. I have vainly laboured under the burden of my family. I have never gone to places of pilgrimage. I have fattened by hands, body and feet. I have never served the Saints. I have never given anything in charity. I have never worshipped any deities. I have hugged to my heart things which I should have avoided. I have done many unjust and unrighteous things. I have not known the way to real good. I cannot even speak or remember the things that I have done. I have been an enemy to myself, and have committed self-slaughter. Thou art an ocean of compassion, O God! Enable me to cross this worldly existence" (Abg. 4066).

Tukārāma's Sin Stands Between Himself and God

28. Tukārāma thinks that his constant sin stands between himself and God. "I pant after Thy vision and even seek Thy compassion—but it seems that my sin stands between Thee and me. I pursue the devotional path as if by compulsion. . . . I do not know when Thou mayest give composure to my mind" (Abg. 1486). "I came to Thee as a fond child, but my desires were not fulfilled. I follow Thee as under necessity, but my endeavour stops in the middle. It seems my sin has become powerful, and stands as an obstacle in my vision of Thy feet" (Abg. 2835). "New sins attack me while I try to surrender myself to Thee. Be Thou compassionate, O God. Why should anything have any sway over us, when we try to follow Thee?" (Abg. 2759). "Do not count my faults. I am sin incarnate. I am sinful, Thou art holy. I am a sinner, Thou art a redeemer. The sinner may do his deeds, but the redeemer must come to his help. If an iron hammer tries to beat down a Parisa, the Parisa will turn the hammer into one of gold. Nobody cares for a clod of earth; but it becomes valuable when it comes in contact with musk" (Abg. 1458). This same idea Tukārāma expresses elsewhere when he says that it may be his to sin, but it is God's to save him. "Do not fail to do Thy duty, O compassionate God! It becomes us to commit sins, but it becomes Thee to succour the unholy. I have done my duty, and it behooves Thee to discharge Thine. Do not fail to accomplish Thy traditional task," says Tukā (Abg. 1223).

The Reasons Why Probably God Does Not Show Himself to Tukārāma

29. Tukārāma next goes on to discuss the reasons why probably God does not show Himself to him. In the first place, he says that he probably lacks sufficient endeavour, and the grit of body and mind which alone enables one to reach God. He is therefore thrown in a great doubt as to whether God may ever show Himself to him. "Whether Thou wilt ever accept me or not,—that gives me food for thought. Whether Thou wilt show Thy feet to me or not,—that makes my mind unsteady. Whither Thou wilt ever speak with me or not,—that puts anxiety into my mind. Whether Thou wilt remember me or not,—that puts me in a state of doubt. Probably," says Tukā, "Thou dost not accept me, because I lack sufficient endeavour" (Abg. 3299). A second reason, probably, which, according to Tukā, makes God not to show Himself to him, is that God may suppose that he may ask something of Him when He has shown Himself to Tukā. Tukārāma tells God that he would ask nothing of Him, if God condescends to show Himself to him. "Anything which will put my Lord into difficulties,—what will that avail me? I shall not tease Thee, O God, or ask anything of Thee. I have from the bottom of my heart left off all ambition for power, or success, or wealth, or even absolution. I only want Thee to show Thyself to me but once, and clasp me to Thy bosom" (Abg. 3019). Probably also, says Tukā, God does not show Himself to him, because, he has not yet completely resigned himself to His will. "I have given over my body to Thee, and yet I entertain fear. So treacherous am I. Such a great mistake I have committed. What I speak by word of mouth, I have not experienced in my heart. I deserve a severe punishment at Thy hands, O God, for this impropriety" (Abg. 3061).

The Humility of Tukārāma

30. Tukā's mind is tossed at the thought that people praise him for nothing. He invites God, to disillusion him when he regards himself as a great singer. "I think in my mind, O God, that there is no singer like me. Thou are omniscient and great. Shalt Thou not be able to dispel this illusion? Desire and anger have not yet lost their hold on my mind. They have taken a permanent lodgment in me. I have disburdened myself before Thee in order that Thou mayest know my mind" (Abg. 1476). "Of low caste though I may be, yet because Saints have praised me, I feel an internal arrogance. This, I am sure, will end by robbing me of my virtue. I feel internally that I alone am a wise man. Save me," says Tukā; "or otherwise, I shall come to ruin" (Abg. 2072). Tukārāma questions God why He has brought fame to him when he did not deserve it. "What happiness will a man derive when his body is anointed with sandal, if he is feeling a severe ache in his stomach? Why hast Thou brought fame to me, O God? If dainty dishes are served before a man who has had fever, what relish could he have for them? If a dead body be adorned with ornaments, of what use would it be to the body?" (Abg. 1474). With humility, which is a natural product of mystical introspection, Tukārāma describes how with all his poetry he is forever away from God. "A parrot speaks as it is taught. . . . The happiness of a dream does not make one a king. . . . Why shouldst Thou have adorned my tongue with song? For, it takes me away from Thee. Of what use is gold reflected in a mirror? You look at it, but are unable to catch hold of it. . . . A cow-boy tends cattle, but he does not own them" (Abg. 2850). "Good things," says Tukā, "are like poison to me. I do not want either happiness or honour. What should I do to these people who persist in giving that to me? When the body is being tended, I feel as if it were on fire. Good food is like poison. My heart is troubled when I hear my praise. Show me the way to see Thee, set me not to pursue a mirage, do what is ultimately good to me, and take me out of this burning fire" (Abg. 246). "When shall I be made an outcast, O God, in order that in repentance I shall remember Thy feet? Tears will trickle down my eyes, and I shall know no sleep. When shall I be able to enjoy solitude? Help me, O God, to achieve my object" (Abg. 1221).

A Request to the Saints to Intercede

31. Tukārāma found, however, that not by merely living in solitude he would be able to reach God. He needed very much the company of the Saints, who would be able to give him the evangel of God. In a state of utter forlornness, Tukārāma says that there was no townsman for him in this life. His city was planted in heaven, while everybody who talked to him and met him spoke only of earthly things. "I see no townsman for me in this life. How shall I lead a lonely life in this world? I so much pant after spiritual company. Wherever I look, in whatever direction I cast my eyes, I find an empty space everywhere. I feel forlorn, and nobody tells me news of Thee," says Tukā (Abg. 741). If Tukārāma could not find God, he said he should be at least so fortunate as to live in the company of the Saints who would tell him the news of God. "Give me the company of those who have an incessant love towards Thee, O God. Then I shall no longer tease Thee. I shall live near the feet of the Saints and shall ask nothing of Thee. If Thou canst bestow upon me this boon, Thou wilt kill two birds with one stone. Neither Thou nor I shall be teased any longer. For this reason, I am standing like a beggar at Thy door" (Abg. 635). "When I rember the spiritual experience of the Saints, my heart burns within me. I shall offer my life to Thee as a sacrifice, so that Thou mayest make me worthy of the Saints. Words without experience are as valueless as a creeper without fruit. . . . " (Abg. 2915). Moreover, "the Saints, who have seen Thee in bodily form, will laugh at me and count me as unworthy for spiritual life. It is this thought which makes me sad. They have described Thy form in this way and in that way. How shall I be able to describe Thee? . . . Tell me what faults I have committed, and why Thou regardest myself as unworthy. Thou art known to have equal feelings towards all, being their common parent.

Remove my ignorance, O God, by giving me this knowledge. . . . (Abg. 4092). Then, not being able to find God Himself, he appeals to the Saints to tell him whether God will ever favour him. "Shall I be relieved of this miserable existence? Will God favour me? Tell me, O Saints, and give composure to my mind. Can the actions I have done cease to bear fruit? . . . How may I be able to know God's secret? Will my intellect be ever composed? Or will any obstacles come in the way? When shall I reach the end? When shall I be able to throw myself at the feet of God? When will these eyes rejoice at the blessed vision of God? . . . This is what is filling me with anxiety day and night," says Tukā. "I cannot imagine that my unaided strength will ever make me reach the end" (Abg. 4072). "When shall I be able to rejoice in the vision of the God-head among all men? Then my happiness will know no bounds, and I shall merge myself in an ocean of bliss. Then will tranquillity and forgiveness and compassion make lodgment in my soul, and drive away my evil passions. Then shall I shine like a burning fire of dispassion and discrimination. Then shall I be a pattern of nine-fold Bhakti, the crown of all emotions. . . . " (Abg. 1707). "When shall I be able to hear the words of the Saints that Thou hast accepted me? Then alone shall my mind rest at ease. I have made Thy face and feet the cynosure of my eyes. I shall fix myself firmly in the words of the Saints, and I shall do no other Sādhana for meeting Thee. . . . " (Abg. 719). "Do me this charity, O Saints. You are compassionate and holy. Remember me to God, and tell Him the agonies of my heart. I am without a Lord. Faultful, fallen, throw me not away. God shall not leave me, if you but intercede on my behalf," says Tukā (Abg. 1539).

The Asking of Grace From God

32. Tukārāma tries yet another way. He approaches God direct, and feeling his great impotence in reaching God, requests Him to send down His grace on him. What cannot be done by human endeavour, may be accomplished by divine grace. "Throw me not away," says Tukā, "I am a dog at Thy door. I am sitting like a beggar before Thy house. Turn me not out of Thy mansion. I am like an evil thing before Thy presence. Save me by Thy power, O God" (Abg. 2722). "Save me," says Tukā again, "from these all-encompassing and never-ending meshes by Thy Divine power. As I think about it, I find my mind is uncontrollable, and runs after sense. I have taken the bait and cannot throw it out by my own power. Powerless as I am, I am waiting for Thy vision, O God" (Abg. 1452). "I have been verily pent up in this Samsāra as a serpent is pent up within a basket by the music of a juggler. . . . Save me by Thy power. I feel I am impotent to go beyond this enchantment. I have caught the bait like a fish which runs after food, and then kills itself by it. I am like a bird which tries to find its young one, but gets itself caught in a net. Like a fly sticking in a sweet substance, the more I shake my wings, the more I get myself inside. My very life is departing. Save me by Thy power, O God" (Abg. 639). Tukārāma takes resort to other analogies, and requests God to lift him up as a mother lifts up her child. "I have become wearied my Mother, and can walk no longer. Lift me up in Thy kindness and love. Put me to Thy breast, and ward off my hunger which has continued to give me trouble throughout life. I am wearied, and cannot even speak" (Abg. 1406). Then, again, Tukārāma regards himself as a Chātaka bird which is desirous of getting some drops of rain in its beak. It would not partake of any water on earth. It must have water from heaven to satisfy its thirst. "I feel thirsty like a Chātaka bird. Rain Thy grace on me, O God! I am directing my sight towards heaven, and Thou knowest it already. A sprout can grow into a tree only when it is watered from above" (Abg. 2863). "Let me have a vision of Thy feet, as a man after a long-continued fast may have of food. Let love spring in me, as it springs in a child when it sees its mother after a long time. Let covetousness rise in me about God, as it rises in a stingy man when he looks at a treasure," says Tukā (Abg. 1884). Indeed, says Tukārāma, there is no need for him to give vent to his thoughts by word of mouth; for God knows his thoughts already. His only business is to ask compassion of God. . . . His own power is inadequate to reach God, and all sādhanas are useless. We must sacrifice ourselves to God, says Tukā, and cease to think of the end time and again (Abg. 1224). Finally, he invites God to help him, only if his words are a true index to his heart, and if his behaviour does not belie his internal feelings; for God knows all things already (Abg. 1084).

The Centre of Indifference

33. Hitherto, Tukārāma believed it possible for him to have a vision of God. He waited long and tried various means to that end. But nothing would help him. He believed at first fully in his power to know God, but he now began to find it almost impossible for him to know Him. From the everlasting yea, he now began to pass through the centre of indifference. "How long shall I wait," he asks, "I see no sign of God's presence. It seems to me, O God that Thou and I shall have now to part. How long shall I wait? I do not see the fructification of Thy promises." Tukārāma thought that he was ruined both externally and internally. His family life was a failure, and it seemed that his spiritual life was equally so. So far as his family life was concerned, he was at his purse's end, and was to much in debt that nobody would give him any debt any longer. It was impossible for him to go to other men's houses. He had lost all reputation and honour among men for having followed the path of God (Abg. 1260). He was left by his relatives and friends . . . and it seemed that he had lost all shame. . . . He had disgraced himself. It seemed that an evil spirit had taken possession of his intellect, and would not give him any που στῶ. "It was probable," says Tukārāma, "that God had many devotees and left this one in the lurch" (Abg. 1757). Thus, Tukārāma seemed to have been ruined both in worldly and spiritual matters. His desire remained unfulfilled. His mind burned like a seed on a frying pan. Nothing gave satisfaction to his mind. He could not know what was in store for him. He went up and down as if caught in a whirlpool. He was incessantly going up and descending down the mountain of thought (Abg. 3540).

The Everlasting Nay

34. Tukārāma did not stay for a long time in the centre of indifference. He saw no help coming. He began to call in question the omnipotence of God. He thought that even his Fate was more powerful than God. "I have lost all patience," says he, "and Thou hast not accepted me. I think my Fate is more powerful than Thee. I have grown powerless to wend on my way. My cries are of no avail. Tukā does not know how to sacrifice himself to God, and God has thus become indifferent to him" (Abg. 1485). "When people of old realised their spiritual end, they did so by their own power. They strained every nerve in realising Thee. Thou hast merely repaid the obligation which they had conferred on Thee. Thou hast never saved, O God, a powerless being like myself," . . . says Tukā (Abg. 1279). "God's impotence is now proved," says Tukā. "His Name has no power. My love towards Thee is gradually diminishing. Enormous sin stands in the way. My mental agony increases. God has acquired the quality of impotence," says Tukā (Abg. 1923). Then, again, Tukārāma tries another remedy for invoking the attention of God. He tells him that He has forgotten what His devotees have done for Him. It is the devotees that have endowed Him with a form. "It is due to men like us that Thou art made to assume a form and a name. Who else might otherwise have cared for Thee? Thou hast lived in the great Void. Darkness brings lustre to the lamp. The setting brings lustre to the jewel. The patient brings the doctor to light. . . . Poison makes nectar valuable. Brass makes gold have a value. It is due to us," says Tukā, "that Thou art made a God at all" (Abg. 2527). In the same strain Tukārāma says, "Thou hast forgotten that our devotion has endowed Thee with Godhood. Great men are short of memory. They cannot remember unless they are put in mind of a thing. It is due to us that Thou art able to move. In Thine own impersonal form, Thou wouldst not be obliged to do anything of that kind. . . . " (Abg. 2159). God taxed Tukārāma's patience to the utmost. Tukārāma now came to know that Godhood was a meaningless word. Who can now preserve that empty symbol? "Why has God punished me hitherto?" asks Tukā. "Now God and I are placed on an equality. Whatever I may say about Thee, whatever word of abuse I may utter, it all becomes

Thee, O God. Thou art shameless, and without caste, and race. Thou art a thief, and an adulterer. Thou livest upon stones, and mud, . . . animals, and trees. . . . I know that Thou art an ass, and a dog, and an ox, and bear all sorts of burdens. People in by-gone times have known that Thou art a liar. I have come to know the truth of the remark," says Tukā. "Thou hast provoked me to a quarrel, and nobody can now gag my mouth" (Abg. 1531). Elsewhere, he says that God is verily a beggar, and His work a lie. "It is shameless beings like myself that have patience to put their faith in God. . . . God does not speak, and yet accepts all service from His servants" (Abg. 1252). God is not merely a beggar, but makes His devotees beggars like unto Him. Woe to the company of God, says Tukā. "Thou makest Thy servant a beggar like Thyself. Thou hast no name and form. Thou makest Thy devotee even likewise. As Thou hast nothing in Thyself, Thou shalt reduce me to naught" (Abg. 1546). Tukārāma then goes on to shower every kind of abuse on God. He calls God timid, because He does not approach Tukā. "Nobody stands between Thee and me," he says. "Thou art timid to approach me. . . . Being the support of the world, Thou seemest to be powerless. It is we, who give Thee support by uttering Thy name time after time. I have been verily caught," says Tukā, "in the net of the elements" (Abg. 2662). He calls in question the generosity of God, and says that it is a shame to His generosity that He should have made him heter-dependent. "Thou hast made me dependent upon others. . . . Thou art known to be generous, O God. There is an end to Thy generosity now. All my supplications are of no avail, and Thou knowest no charity. Why shouldst Thou have given birth to us at all, O God?" asks Tukā. "Why shouldst Thou have made me an object of pity? Does it not prove Thy impotence?" asks Tukā (Abg. 2776). "I am ashamed to call myself Thy servant. Events belie my words. Thou hast left unfulfilled the words of bygone saints. Thou hast even made me sing. But that seems to be now merely a farce" (Abg. 3447). "How should I call myself Thy servant, if my wishes remain unfulfilled? If Thou carest for my love, do not delay any longer. If Thou hast to show Thyself to me sometime, why dost Thou not do it now? I can sing with justification only when I have seen Thee" (Abg. 1567). "How cruel must God be," asks Tukā, "that He should not have shown Himself to me even though He is reputed to be so near? Thou livest in my heart, and hast no compassion on me. Thou art cruel and impersonal. Thou knowest not the pangs of my heart. My mind knows no rest. My senses wander. My sin is not at an end. Thou art as angry as ever" (Abg. 243). "If Thou dost not show Thyself to me now," says Tukārāma, "Thou shalt receive a curse from me, Thy son. Why art Thou garnering Thy treasure and for whom, if not for us, Thy children? Thou allowest Thy children to cry with hunger. . . . By our curse Thou shalt be ruined, O God. Being my father, Thou shalt be an object of my curse" (Abg. 3548). "I shall spoil Thy fair name, if Thou continuest to be indifferent. . . . I shall refuse to utter Thy name, and shall drown Thy whole lineage" (Abg. 3549). "People will say that from our omnipotent Father we are born impotent. These abuses will be hurled in Thy face by the world, and Thy name shall be dishonoured. . . . I feel my life to be a burden" (Abg. 3550). Tukārāma then went to call in question the very existence of God. He tells Him that he would not have grown mad after Him, had he known already that He did not exist. "Empty is the name that Thou obtainest in the world. . . . In my opinion, God does not exist. . . . My words have fallen short of reality. I have grown hopeless. I have lost both the life of the world and the life of the spirit" (Abg. 3303). Tukārāma ends by saying that in his opinion God is dead. "To me, God is dead. Let Him be for whomsoever thinks Him to be. I shall no longer speak about God. I shall not meditate on His name. Both God and I have perished. . . . Vainly have I followed Him hitherto, and vainly have I spent my life for Him" (Abg. 1597). "Shall I now throw myself on a scimitar or into a flame of fire, or shall I lose myself in a forest and expose myself to the extremes of heat and cold, or shall I close my lips forever? Shall I besmear my body with ashes, or wander like a nomad over the world? Shall I give up the ghost by a long fast? Tell me, O God, the way to find Thee if Thou dost exist" (Abg. 457). And finally, not finding God, Tukārāma determines to commit self-slaughter. "Thou hast no anxiety for me. Why now should I continue to live? . . . I had lived in the vain hope that Thou mightest come to the succour of this sinful creature. Nobody will now accept me, and Thou hast adamantine cruelty. My hopes are shattered, and I shall now commit self-slaughter" (Abg. 2266).

IV. THE ECSTATIC AND POST-ECSTATIC EXPERIENCES OF TUKĀRĀMA

Tukārāma's Sudden Vision of God

35. God could wait no longer. The agonies of Tukārāma had reached an extreme stage, and his heart-rending cry was heard by God. The dark cloud on Tukārāma's heart was now suddenly illumined by the flashes of God's vision. As happens in the case of all mystics, the dark night was suddenly relieved by the great light that followed. Tukārāma saw God's vision and bowed at His feet. "I see God's face, and the vision gives me infinite bliss. My mind is riveted on it, and my hands cling to His feet. As I look at Him, all my mental agony vanishes. Bliss is now leading me to an ever higher bliss," says Tukā (Abg. 1329). "Blessed am I that my effort has been crowned with success. I have attained the desired end. My heart is set on God's feet, and my mind is composed. The blessed omen has wiped off death and old age. . . . My body is changed. On it has fallen the light of God. I have now obtained limitless wealth, and I have seen the feet of the formless Person. I have obtained a treasure which has existed from times immemorial. . . . For my very life, I will never leave it any longer. Let no evil eye affect my possession," says Tukā (Abg. 4065).

Reasons According to Tukā for His Realisation of God

36. When Tukārāma looked back to find out the reasons which had led him to realise God, he found, in the first place, that the company of the Saints had been mainly responsible for this happy consummation. "My fortune has brightened and my anxiety has been at an end on account of the company of the Saints. By their favour have I been able to find out God. I shall now enclose Him in the chest of my heart. That hidden treasure has been found out by my devotion" (Abg. 449). In the second place, Tukārāma says that the realisation of God was due entirely to the descent of God's grace on him without any merit on his own part. "Suddenly has the treasure been placed in my hands, and fact, without any adequate service. My fate has become powerful, and I have seen God. Never more shall there be any loss to me, and my poverty is gone. My anxieties are at an end, and I have been the most fortunate of men. . . . " (Abg. 1775). Tukārāma, however, is not entirely unconscious of the great effort that he had made for God-realisation. "In all ways, however, I tried to reach this consummation. I conscientiously did service to my Lord. I never looked back. I conquered time by utilising every moment. I did not disturb my mind by conjectures, nor did I allow any evil desires to come in the way. . . . Now that fortune has smiled on me, I shall move on undaunted" (Abg. 1673). Lastly, Tukārāma says that God has accepted him, probably on account of his defects. "God accepted me seeing that I was a man of low birth, a man without intellect, a man of humble and mean form, and with other bad things about me. I have now come to know that whatever God does ultimately conduces to our good. I have enjoyed infinite bliss. . . . " Tukā says that God is proud of His name, and therefore comes to the succour of His devotees (Abg. 691).

A Confession of Blessedness

37. Tukārāma now feels satisfied that his long effort has come to an end, and that now he would be able to enjoy the company of God to his heart's content. "For long had I waited to see Thy feet. Time had parted us for a long time. Now shall I enjoy Thy company to my satisfaction. Desires hitherto had given me much trouble. . . . I was long moving away from the path. . . . For long was I merged in mere semblance. . . . Now the consummation has been reached, and I am merged in enjoyment" (Abg. 2322). Tukārāma asks God to stop and look at him. "I never cared for my relatives, I moved after Thee in order that Thou mightest speak with me. I had waited long to enjoy Thy company in solitude. Stand, O God, before me and look at me," says Tukā (Abg. 1610). "How blessed am I that I have seen Thy feet to-day! How much have the Saints done for me, O God! To-day's gain is indescribable. Its auspiciousness is beyond measure. Tukā wonders how so great a fortune should have fallen to his lot" (Abg. 2005). "All the quarters have now become auspicious to me. Evil has itself been transformed into the highest good. The lamp in my hand has dispelled all darkness. . . . The grief I hitherto felt will now conduce to happiness. I now see goodness in all created things" (Abg. 1310). "Blessed am I that my love has been fixed in Thy name. My blessedness is undoubted. I shall never be a creature to the onslaught of time. I shall now live on the spiritual nectar, and live always in the company of the Saints. Satisfaction is being added to satisfaction, and enjoyment to enjoyment" (Abg. 1098). Tukārāma now considers that everyday to him is a holiday. "Blessedness beyond compare! . . . We, who are mad after God, are sunk in blessedness. We shall sing and dance and clap our hands, and please God. Every day to me is now a holiday. We are full of joy, and the omnipotent God will vindicate us in every way. . . ." (Abg. 3998). "I have become entirely careless of the objects of sense. Divine joy is seething through my body. My tongue has become uncontrollable, and ceaselessly utters the name of God. From greater to greater bliss do I go, as a miser goes from greater to greater riches. All my emotions have been unified in God, as the rivers in an ocean" (Abg. 975). "And no wonder that people will reckon me," says Tukā, "as more blessed than any other being. Those who boast of self-knowledge, and those who boast of absolution will both lose colour before me. My very body becomes divine when I sing the praise of God. Fortunate am I that God is my debtor. To a man who goes on pilgrimages, I shall bring weariness; and to one who seeks the enjoyment of heaven, I shall bring disgust. . . . Blessed will people call me," says Tukā; "blessed are we, they will say, that we have seen Tukā" (Abg. 3598).

Tukārāma is a Photic as Well as an Audile Mystic

38. Tukārāma was a photic as well as an audile mystic, like all the other great mystics of the world. This is evident from the way in which he describes his light and sound experiences. "The whole world has now become alight, and darkness is at an end. There is no space for me to hide myself. . . . The day of Truth has come, and its spread is now beyond measure. For the sake of his life," says Tukā, "he has won his goal" (Abg. 2556). "God," he says, "shines like a diamond set in a circle of rich jewels. His light is like the light of a million moons. . . . " Tukā says that His vision is now satisfied, and refuses to return from its cynosure (Abg. 4026). It is impossible for him, says Tukārāma elsewhere, to describe the bliss of unceasing illumination. "Thou art our kind and affectionate mother, O God, and bearest all our burdens. We know no fear, nor any anxiety. . . . I cannot know the night from day, and the unceasing illumination exists at all times. How shall I be able to describe the great bliss I enjoy? I have worn the ornaments of Thy names, and by Thy power nothing is lacking to me" (Abg. 4083). Tukārāma also describes how he was hearing the mystic sound all the while. "God has really favoured me" he says. "My doubts and delirium are at an end. God and Self are now lying on the same couch in me. Tukārāma now sleeps in his own Form, and mystic bells lull him to sleep" (Abg. 3252). "I have been in tune with the Infinite, and psychical dispositions take time to emerge. I have become full of spiritual pride, and I cannot control my limbs. Another voice speaks through me, and happiness and sorrow have lost their difference. I can hardly find words to describe the happiness to these people.They may wonder at it, and say this is impossible. Both my exterior and interior are filled with Divine bliss," says Tukā (Abg. 1039).

Tukārāma's Other Mystical Experiences

39. Tukārāma elsewhere describes his other mystical experiences also. In one place, he tells us, "God is pursuing me outright. I have fallen in the hands of God," he says, "and He is using me as a menial without wages. He extracts work from me, not caring what condition it may bring me into. Wherever I go, God pursues me. He has deprived me of all my possessions," says Tukā (Abg. 2612). Elsewhere he tells us that God is moving all around him. "I have been pent up internally and externally by God. He has put an end to all my work, and has deprived me even of my mind. He has deprived me of self-hood, and has separated me from all things. In close connection with me," says Tukā, "He is moving round and round" (Abg. 3810). Tukārāma orders God to stand before him, so long as he is looking at Him. "I like immensely this form of Thine; and my eyes are satisfied. My mind having caught the bait of Your vision, does not leave it on any account. . . . " (Abg. 3111). Tukārāma tells us also that wherever he goes, God is there to walk by him, and help him on his way by taking up his hand. "It is by Thy support that I move on the way. Thou bearest all my burden. Thou puttest meaning into my meaningless words. Thou hast taken away my shame, and put courage into me. . . . " (Abg. 1307). He tells us also that God and he himself are forever interlocked. "Thy hand is on my head, and my heart is on Thy feet. Thus have we been interlocked body into body, self into self. It is mine to serve, and Thine to favour," says Tukā (Abg. 2761).

Tukārāma's Self-vision

40. The highest experience, however, of which a mystic is capable, occurs, as Tukārāma says in another passage, when the difference between Self and God has vanished. "I gave birth to myself, and came out of my own womb," says Tukā. "All my desires are at an end, and my end is achieved. When I became powerful beyond measure, I died at the very moment. Tukā looks on both sides, and sees Himself by himself" (Abg. 3944). When Tukārāma saw Himself, nothing remained for him to be achieved. "God is the giver, and God is the enjoyer. What else remains to be experienced? Or, how can we put it into words? By the eyes I see my own form. The whole world seems to be filled by Divine music," says Tukā (Abg. 179). Finally, Tukārāma finds himself pent up all around by his own Self. "Deep has called unto deep, and all things have vanished into unity. The waves and the ocean have become one. Nothing can come, and nothing can now pass away. The self is enveloping Himself all around. The time of the Great End has come, and sunset and sunrise have ceased" (Abg.

1815). In this way, Tukārāma describes how his self had merged in God.

The Effects of God-vision

41. The very first effect of God-vision, says Tukārāma, is that God has made him mad. "He follows me wherever I go, and makes it impossible for me to forget Him. He has robbed away my heart which was all my treasure. He has shown Himself to my vision, and made me go mad after Him. My mouth refuses to speak, and my ears to hear. . . . My whole body has been filled by the heat of Divine passion," says Tukā (Abg. 1059). "My previous outlook," says Tukā, "has been entirely changed on account of the new possession. I find no life now in worldly life. A new possession of the soul has taken place. The former outlook has changed. My life has been filled with divine joy. The tongue has partaken of a new sweetness, God's name is fixed in my mouth, and my mind has become tranquil. . . . Whatever I wish, shall now be fulfilled wherever I am," says Tukā (Abg. 2623). God's vision has next deprived Tukā of solitude. "Where can I run, being afraid of this worldly life? Wherever I look, God is present. He has deprived me of solitude, and there is no place without Him. How shall I say that I am going to another place? When a sleeping man awakes, he finds himself in his home. What do I owe Thee, O God, that Thou hast penned me from all sides?" (Abg. 1197). Tukārāma tells us that God speaks to him whenever he wants an answer. "Look at my spiritual experience," says Tukā. "I have possessed God. Whatever I speak, God fulfils. Whatever I ask, God answers immediately. When I left off this worldly life, God became my servant. It is due to my patience, says Tukā, that I have been able to possess God" (Abg. 2260). Tukārāma asks God whatever his mind desires. "I shall now throw all my burden upon Thee. When I feel hungry, I shall ask for food. When I experience cold, I shall ask for clothing. Whatever my mind desires, I shall ask it of Thee at the very moment. Sorrow shall never attack our house. The great disc in Thy hand moves round about us, and wards off all evil. I have no care for absolution," says Tukā. "I long for this worldly existence" (Abg. 2513). The mystic sees not, says Tukā, and yet he sees. "I have not seen anything, and yet I see everything. I and mine have been removed from me. I have taken without taking, I have eaten without eating, spoken without speech. Whatever has been hidden, has been brought to light. I never heard, and yet all things have sauntered into my mind," says Tukā (Abg. 118). And thus is happens that Tukārāma is merely a looker-on. "There is now no work for me. All at once, every kind of work has been taken away. I will now sit silent at a place, and do whatever I like. The world vainly follows illusions. All of a sudden," says Tukā, "I have been out of the world" (Abg. 850). He has been free from all connections whatsoever. "I do not belong to any place; I belong only to one place. I do not move out, and come back. . . . There is no difference to me between mine and thine. I do not belong to anybody. I am not required to be born and to die. I am as I am. There is neither name nor form for me, and I am beyond action and inaction," says Tukā (Abg. 256).

The Whole Universe Becomes God

42. "All men have now become God," says Tukā, "and merit and demerit have disappeared. . . . My mind has been filled with great happiness. When one looks into a mirror, it seems as if one is looking at a different object, and yet one is looking at oneself. When a brook runs into a river, it becomes merged in it" (Abg. 2281). "My country is now the universe," says Tukā. "I live in the whole world. All the people in the world have come to know that I am dear to my Father. There is nobody between Him and me; there is no chasm. My only resting place is the Name of God" (Abg. 1113). "If I mean to worship Thee," says Tukā, "such worship becomes impossible, as Thou art identical with all means of worship. Tell me, O God, how I may worship Thee. If I may give Thee ablution of water, Thou are that Thyself. Thou art the scent of scents, and the fragrance of flowers. . . . If I am to place Thee on a couch, Thou art Thyself that. Thou art all the food that may be offered to Thee. If I am to sing a song, Thou art that song. If I sound the cymbals, Thou art those. There is no place whereon I could now dance. The scent and the light are now Rāma, Kṛishṇa, Hari" (Abg. 1128). "I see Thy feet everywhere. The whole universe is filled by Thee. . . . Thou hast become everything to us, says Tukā. We have no taste for work or worldly life. We need not go anywhere or do anything. We utter Thy name and meditate on Thee. Whatever I speak is a recitation of Thy qualities. . . . When I walk, I turn round about Thee. When I sleep, I fall prostrate before Thee. . . . All wells and rivers are now Thyself. All houses, and palaces have now become the temples of God. Whatever I hear is the name of God. Various sounds are heard," says Tukā, "we are the servants of God, and are ever filled with great joy" (Abg. 1228).

The Signs of God's Presence in the Soul

43. What are the marks by which a Saint may be known? "He to whose house God comes," says Tukā, "loses his manhood. When God comes to live in a man, He deprives him of everything except Himself. The marks of God's presence are that He allows no desires in a Saint, nor any affection. . . . He, who has come to know God, becomes garrulous, and yet is never tainted by untruth. . . . All these marks may be seen in me," says Tukā (Abg. 2583). He tells us furthermore that women to him appear as bears, and gold as a clod of earth. "I never like anything in this world except the Name of God. Mortal existence seems to me to be a vomit. Gold and silver are like a clod of earth. Jewels appear like stones. Beautiful women," says Tukā, "appear to us like bears" (Abg. 224). The Saint can know no fear, says Tukārāma. "Is it possible for a man to find out darkness by means of a lamp? Similarly, we, who are the servants of God, shall never be afraid of death and other mirages. An unfortunate man does not know that the Sun cannot be hidden by dust. Fire can never be hidden by grass," says Tukā (Abg. 258). A Saint in all his actions gives constant lodgment to God. "Whatever he sees is God, whatever he speaks is God. . . . The whole body becomes filled by God, and passions forever take leave of me," says Tukā (Abg. 3942). Another mark is the utter self-surrender of the Saint. "I have for once surrendered myself at Thy feet. What more shall I surrender? . . .

I do not see, O God, that there is anything else that I may surrender. . . . " (Abg. 245). He need no longer ask compassion from God. "So long as I was not awakened to this spiritual life, I bore all kinds of grief. But because I am now wakened by the Saints, I know that all things are vain" (Abg. 192). No supplication is now needed, says Tukā. By the power of God, he has got control over events. "We, the servants of God, are not like other men to supplicate to others. By the power of God, the whole world looks dwarfish to us. Time and death are in our hands. God will justify us, His servants. We have surrendered ourselves to Him, and live at his feet. Whatever we now desire, God shall certainly fulfil for us" (Abg. 2296). Tukārām says he has conquered time by resigning all sorrow in God. "I shall meditate on Thee and play about Thee. My heart is set on Thy feet. Thou knowest my heart, O God; no false description of it would be of any use. We have resigned our happiness and sorrow in Thee. We have lost bodily egoism, and the distinction between self and not-self has been effaced" (Abg. 2647). Tukārāma tells us also that he has planted his foot on the forehead of Death. "Death eats up the world but we have planted our foot on his forehead. He will stand up when we shall dance with joy, and will himself come to our help. He whose hunger could never be fulfilled, is now satisfied by God's name. Hot-burning as he was, he has now become cool" (Abg. 1393). Finally, he tells us that both night and sleep had become to him as good as non-existent. He feels that there is no night, because he sees the lustre of God at all times. He cannot sleep, because God's presence always keeps him awake. "Both night and sleep have now departed. I live in God in continual spiritual bliss. God is everywhere and 'me' and 'mine' have departed. God and myself shall now live together, and never shall we be separated" (Abg. 2866).

Tukārāma Sees His Death with His Own Eyes

44. Tukārāma speaks of having seen his death with his own eyes. This means that when he had realised God, his body was dead. "I saw my death with my own eyes. Incomparably glorious was the occasion.

The whole universe was filled with joy, I became everything, and enjoyed everything. I had hitherto stuck to only one place, being pent up by egoism. By my deliverance from it, I am enjoying the harvest of bliss. Death and birth are now no more. I am free from the littleness of 'me' and 'mine.' God has given a place for me to live, and I am proclaiming God to the world" (Abg. 1897). In another passage, he speaks of the funeral pyre of the living body. "The living body is dead, and has been placed in the cemetery. Passions are crying that their lord is gone, and death is crying that he has lost his control. The fire of illumination is burning the body with the fuel of dispassion. The pitcher of egoism is whirled round the head, and is broken to pieces. The death-cry 'I am God' emerges vociferously. The family lineage has been cut off, and the body is delivered to Him who is its Lord. Tukārāma says that when the body was being reduced to ashes, the lamp of the Guru's compassion was burning on it" (Abg. 1896). This death, says Tukā, has brought on everlasting light. "When the body was emptied, God came to inhabit it. . . . By my bodily death, the unending light began to burn. At one stroke, Tukā became non-existent, and his personality came to an end" (Abg. 2637). "When I died," he says elsewhere, "I made over my body to God. Whom and how shall I now serve? The doll throws out its hands and feet, as the wire-puller moves the thread. I speak as God makes me speak. . . . Merit and demerit do not belong to me. They belong to God. Believe me," says Tukā, "I am beyond this body" (Abg. 2160). "My end is gained, my heart is set on Thy name, and infinite joy springs from the remembrance of Thy feet. The purpose for which I had taken on a body has been achieved, and a future life is cut off. A sudden profit has now accrued, and nothing remains to be achieved" (Abg. 1314).

Tukārāma's Great Spiritual Power

45. Tukārāma employs various images to describe his great spiritual power after God-realisation. He speaks of himself as the son of God, and God as his father, and as such he tells us the son must necessarily inherit the patrimony of his father. Then he speaks of himself as being the key-holder of the treasury of God. Thirdly, he speaks of God's grace as the harvest, and himself as the distributor of it. Lastly, he speaks of himself as the Spiritual King of the world. In all these ways he describes how he comes to have sovereign power. To quote Tukārāma, he tells us, in the first place, that he would no longer be a powerless, casteless, mean man. His father is God Pāṇḍuraṅga, and his mother is Rakhumāī. In both ways, he has descended of pure stock. He would no longer be of poor spirit or of dwarfish power. He would no longer be wicked or unfortunate. God would come to his succour. . . . He tells us, furthermore, that death would hide himself before him, and as the rich treasure has come to his lot, he would remain careless in mind (Abg. 1091). He asks in another place,—Who could prevent the son from obtaining the patrimony of his father? "All power and fortune seek the house of the Saints. Who could prevent the son from obtaining the treasure of his father? I would sit on the lap of God," says Tukā, "and there remain fearless and content" (Abg. 859). "The father," he tells us yet in another place, "treasures riches merely for the sake of his son. He gives himself utmost trouble, bears the burden of his son, and makes him the master of his treasury. He puts ornaments on his son, and is satisfied by looking at him. He prevents people from troubling his son, and in so doing does not care even for his own life" (Abg. 2414). Secondly, Tukārāma speaks of himself as being the key-holder of God's treasury. "I shall now give and take by my own power. There is nobody who can prevent me from doing so. I possess, the key of God's treasury, and every kind of merchandise that may be asked for is with me. By the power of my faith, God has made me a free master," says Tukā (Abg. 2386). Thirdly, he speaks of himself as distributing the rich harvest of God, and when the distribution is no longer needed, he would treasure up the remainder. "There is no deficit here," says Tukā. "All castes may come and take away to their satisfaction. The surface of a mirror shows a man as he is. Those who believe in God enjoy solitude even in company, and God comes upon us as a rich harvest. Tukā is the distributor of it, and gives to all as they like" (3946). "And now I shall treasure up the harvest. I shall keep with me the seed of all existence from which all beings spring. I have blown off the chaff, and kept intact the rich grain. To my lot," says Tukā, "God has fallen by the power of my desert" (Abg. 3947). Lastly, in almost the same strain, Tukā speaks of himself as being a crowned spiritual king. "My lineage has been found out, and (as at the coronation of a king) been proclaimed before all. In order to continue the spiritual tradition, I have been crowned king of the spiritual world. The white umbrella now unfurls itself; the banner of the super-conscious state flutters in the air; the mystic sound fills the universe. The Lord of Tukārāma places him on His own spiritual pedestal, and the whole world is filled with joy" (Abg. 3255). And as the spiritual king of the world, Tukā asks, is he not the master of all he wishes? "In the bosom of Bhakti, there are mines of rich jewels, and all things whatsoever are in God. . . . When a king demands anything, nobody says 'nay.' By the power of his faithful service, a servant is himself raised to the position of a master. . . . From his lofty throne, he can now look below upon the world. Tukā was at once placed on the spiritual throne by the power of his faith, and people regarded him as God himself" (Abg. 788).

The Words of Tukārāma are the Words of God

46. As a result of his identification with God, Tukārāma tells us in many places in his Abhaṅgas that God is speaking through him, or that his words are mixed with divinity. "I know nothing, and what I am speaking are not my words, O Saints. Be not angry with me. These are not my words. God Pāṇḍuraṅga speaks through me, as He has filled every nook and cranny of me. How can a foolish man like myself have the power to speak what transcends the Vedas? I only know how to lisp the name of God. By the power of my Guru, God is bearing all my burden" (Abg. 1188). He invites people to believe in him though unlearned; because he bears the impress of Viṭṭhala. "If the holy waters of the Ganges flow past an idle man, should not the other people bathe in those waters? If the wish-cow stands in the court-yard of a pariah, should not the Brahmins make adoration to it? If a man, struck with leucoderma, holds gold in his hands, should not people touch it, considering it unholy? If the Patel of a village is an outcast, should not his words be obeyed? Tukā, in whom devotion has become strong, bears the stamp of Viṭṭhala, and those who do not listen to him, shall have their faces besmirched" (Abg. 3157). "People do not see," says Tukārāma, "that God is speaking through me. I am made to speak words of realisation by God Himself. Unbelieving and unintelligent men cannot know this. These unheard-of gracious words are the gift of God. People cannot come to believe this, even though I tell them so often and often" (Abg. 2353). "As for myself," he says, "I speak only as I am taught by my Master. I do not speak my words. My words are of my gracious Lord. The parrot speaks as it is taught by its master. What can an insignificant man like myself say, unless he is made to speak by the all-supporting Lord? Who can know His ways?" asks Tukā. "He can make a lame man walk without feet" (Abg. 2163). "I have no intellect," Tukārāma tells us. "I speak straight on. I speak merely the words which have been used by the Saints. . . . I cannot even properly utter the name of Viṭṭhala. What then do I know of spiritual knowledge? . . . I was born of a low caste. I cannot speak much. The Lord makes me speak, and He alone knows the innermost meaning of my words" (Abg. 518). "Do not say that I am responsible for my poems. God makes me sing. . . . I am merely set to measure the corn: the corn belongs to my Lord. I am only a servant of my Lord, and hold in my hands His impress and authority" (Abg. 605). "My words are surely mixed with divinity. I do not grope in darkness. I go on sowing in faith. The treasure belongs to my Lord. What room is there for egosim here? I go on awakening people to their duty," says Tukā (Abg. 771). "My speech," Tukārāma also tells us, "is like rain—universal in nature. The thief harbours perpetual fear in his heart. . . . What may we do to this? My words touch the wounds in the hearts of people. He who has the wound will suffer from the probe" (Abg. 1939).

The Mission of Tukārāma

47. Tukārāma had achieved the end of his life, and he now lived only for the benefaction of the world. He had realised, that, like God, he was smaller than an atom and larger than the universe. He had belched out the body and the universe. He had transcended the three stages of consciousness, and was living in the fourth, as a lamp may silently shine in a pitcher. He said that his only business now was the benefaction and betterment of the world (Abg. 3340). His duty was only to spread religion. "To advance religion and to destroy atheism is my business now. . . . I take pointed answers in my hands, and send them like arrows. I have no consideration, says Tukā, of great and small" (Abg. 1445). Tukārāma is conscious that he has been doing this work through various lives. "Through various lives I have been doing this duty, namely, to relieve the oppressed from the sorrows of existence. I shall sing the praises of God, and gather together His Saints. I shall evoke tears even from stones. I shall utter the holy name of God, and shall dance and clap my hands in joy. I shall plant my foot on the forehead of death. I shall imprison my passions and make myself the lord of the senses" (Abg. 1585). He tells us that false prophets will have their sway only so long as they have not seen Tukā. "A jackal will make a noise only so long as he has not seen a lion. The ocean will roar only so long as it has not met the sage Agastya. Dispassion may be spoken of only so long as a beautiful maiden has not been seen. People will speak of bravery only so long as they have not met a born warrior. Rosaries and bodily marks will have their sway, only so long as their bearers have not met Tukā" (Abg. 2011). "Pebbles will shine only so long as the diamond is not brought forth. Torches will shine only so long as the Sun has not risen. People will speak of the Saints only so long as they have not met Tukā" (Abg. 2012). Tukārāma tells us furthermore that he has been a companion of God from of old. "We have been the companions of God from times immemorial. God has taken us along with Him. There has never been any difference between God and ourselves. We have never lived apart from one another. When God was sleeping, I was there. When God took Laṅkā, I was there. When God tended the cattle, I was there. Our business is the meditation of God's name without a moment's respite" (Abg. 1584). Tukā was present, he says, even when Śuka went to the mountains to attain Samādhi. "Spiritual arrogance pursued Śuka. Vyāsa sent him to Janaka in order to remove his pride. Janaka pointed the way to him and sent him to the peak of Meru.Tukā says that he was present even at the time when Śuka attained Samādhi" (Abg. 1717). Thus it happens, says Tukārāma, that he has been living through various incarnations, and as before, even in this life, has come to separate the wheat from the chaff. "I have come to illumine the ways, and to distinguish the true from the false. God makes me speak, being always in my company. By the power of the Lord, I have no fear in my heart. Before me, no tinsel can have any power" (Abg. 176). Tukārāma tells people that he has come in God's name to carry them over the sea of life. "I have girdled up my loins, and have found out a way for you across the ocean of life. Come here, come here, great and small, women and men. Take no thought, and have no anxiety. I shall carry all of you to the other shore. I come as the sole bearer of the stamp of God to carry you over in God's name" (Abg. 221). Tukārāma charges people to cease from doing wrong henceforth. "For whatever has happened hitherto through ignorance, I forgive you all. But do not commit any sins henceforth. He, who commits adultery with another man's wife, has made intercourse with his own mother. He, who does not listen to us, should never come to us. Be on your guard," says Tukā, "and listen when I promise" (Abg. 146). "Your sins will be washed away if you do not commit them again. Utter the name of Viṭṭhala, and you will be free from your sins. Sins shall have no existence before the power of God's name. Millions of sinful acts will be burnt in the fire of God's name. Do not look backwards. . . . I stand guarantee for your sins. Commit as many sins as you can name. Death will have no sway before the fire of God's name" (Abg. 106). "I enjoy this sweet ambrosia and distribute it among men. Do not wander among the woods. Come here and partake of my offer. Your desires shall be fulfilled, if your intellect is fastened on His feet. I come as a meṣsenger from Viṭṭhala. Easy will be the Pathway by which you may go to God" (Abg. 198). Finally, Tukārāma tells us that having had his station originally in heaven, he came down to the earth, like the Saints of old, to pursue the path of Truth. "We will cleanse the path of the Saints. People have ignorantly gone to woods and forests. . . . The true meaning of the Sacred Books has been hidden. Wordy knowledge has been the cause of ruin. Senses have stood in the way of Sādhana. We will ring the bell of Bhakti. It will send a threat into the heart of Death. Rejoice," says Tukā, "in the victorious name of God" (Abg. 222).

CHAPTER 2

Tukārāma's Mystical Teaching

V. PREPARATION FOR MYSTIC LIFE

Introductory

48. Hitherto we have considered Tukārāma's career as it is found in his own writings. Evidently, there is a personalistic colouring to the mystical development of Tukārāma as we have discussed it till now. We shall now proceed to consider the mystical teaching of Tukārāma. This is valuable as coming from Tukārāma when he had reached the stage of a full-fledged Saint. As we have hitherto discussed what Tukārāma said about his own mystical development personally, we shall now discuss what he says of mystical development in general. We shall first consider what preparation Tukārāma considers necessary for mystical realisation.

Rules for the Life of the Novice in Yoga

49. In the first place, Tukārāma teaches how the novice in Yoga should modulate his life, so as ultimately to be able to reach God. He tells us that the novice in Yoga should always be indifferent to all things, should not get himself contaminated internally or externally by anything whatsoever. He should leave off greediness, conquer sleep, take a measured quantity of food, and should, in private or in public, avoid, on pain of death, conversation with women. He alone who believes in such a Sādhana, says Tukā, will ultimately reach the end of his endeavour by the grace of his Guru (Abg. 2068). Such a novice in Yoga should take only such clothing and food as would be sufficient for life, should live in a hermitage either in a far-off cave or in a forest, . . . should not sit talking among men, should carefully guard his senses by the force of his intellect, should make the best use of every moment of his life, and remember God (Abg. 933). It was for this reason that Tukārāma tells us that the Ṛishis of old avoided the world, . . . made subsistence on onions and roots of trees, lived in utter silence, shut their eyes, and meditated on God (Abg. 521). "If we carry on our spiritual practice regularly, what can it not achieve?" asks

Tukā. "The wet root of a plant breaks even huge rocks. Practice can achieve anything whatsoever. Nothing can stand in the way of a determined effort. A rope can cut a hard stone. One can get oneself accustomed to poison by taking it in increasingly large doses. A child carves a place for itself in the mother's womb as time elapses" (Abg. 848). "Have not people taken large quantities of aconite," asks Tukā, "by gradually accustoming themselves to it? One can take a poisonous snake in his hands, striking terror into the hearts of the on-lookers. Through practice," says Tukā, "even the impossible becomes possible" (Abg. 159). "Thus we should go to solitude and fix our mind on God, should not allow our mind to wander, should avoid all frivolity, . . . should set our heart on reality, and pierce it as an arrow pierces the mark. We should bid good-bye to idleness and to sleep, and live in the constant wakefulness of God" (Abg. 2865).

The Worldly Life of the Spiritual Aspirant

50. Tukārāma's advice to the man who wishes to accomplish both Prapañcha and

Paramārtha at the same time, that is to say, to seek the worldly and the spiritual life together, is, that by doing so, he would lose them both. "He who says that he would accomplish the worldly and the spiritual life together, shall accomplish neither. Between two stones he will only fall to the ground. He will be ruined on both sides, and will ultimately go to hell" (Abg. 3144). The novice in Yoga, therefore, should, in the first place, ward off all relatives, whether son or wife or brother. "When we have once known that they are ultimately of no use, why should we get ourselves contaminated by them? We should break a pitcher for them, as one breaks for a dead body. . . . " (Abg. 81). "If our father and mother happen to create obstacles in our spiritual life, we should ward them off. Who cares for wife and children and wealth? They are merely a source of sorrow. . . . Prahlāda left off his father, Bibhīshaṇa his brother, Bharata both his mother and kingdom. The feet of God alone," says "Tukā, are our final resort; everything else is a source of evil" (Abg. 83). This is the negative social ethics which Tukārāma preaches for the initial stages of the spiritual life. "Such a man should take thought as to the real way of deliverance from mortal life. If one gets drowned in a boat made of stones, who can save him? One should not therefore destroy oneself like a fly jumping into a flame. If a man takes quantities of arsenic, he should not call for a doctor in his last moment" (Abg. 4002). "Such a man should throw away the frivolities of life, and follow the path by which have gone the Saints of old. He should gradually unwind the skein of worldly life. He should follow the footprints of those who have gone ahead. . . . He should think time after time about his past conduct, and take courage for the future, Tukā says that as a man speaks, so he must live" (Abg. 1399). "He should not fill his vision with the evanescence of the world. He should consider that the mortal body is destined to perish, and that Death is eating it up every moment. He should seek company of the Saints, and make haste for the spiritual life. He should not allow his eyes to be blinded by the smoke of worldly existence" (Abg. 2339). "He should eat the leaves of trees, and sing Viṭṭhala time after time.

He should wear bark-garments, and leave off bodily egoism. He should consider honour among men as good as vomit, and live in solitude for the sake of God. He should not go in for complacency of conduct, but live in a forest. He, who determines to carry on his life in this way," says Tukā, "will reach the goal of his life" (Abg. 2999). His final advice, so far as this kind of negative ethics is concerned, is that one should never hope to carry on Prapañcha and Paramārtha together. "When one goes to a menagerie of buffaloes, one gets only eaten-up straw. He who expects to get good sleep on a couch filled with bugs is a fool. A drunken man is sure some day to rave naked," says Tukā (Abg. 1008).

Moral Precepts for the Spiritual Aspirant

51. Tukārāma advises the spiritual aspirant to regard another man's wife as his mother, to avoid censure of others, to throw away lust for other people's wealth, to sit at a place and meditate on God, to believe in the Saints, and to tell the truth. By these means, says Tukā, one can reach God (Abg. 36). He elsewhere enumerates the obstacles in the way of spiritual life as being the flattery of men, the bargaining of money for spiritual matters, lust for another man's wife and wealth, hatred towards beings, egoism of the body, and forgetfulness of God. These he asks God to prevent from attacking him (Abg. 1867). "Some people," he says, "tease their body uselessly for the sake of spiritual realisation. They wear brown clothes; but a dog is also brown. They bear matted hair; but a bear also has got matted hair. They live in caves; but even rats live in caves. These people," says Tukā, "tease their bodies for nothing" (Abg. 2982). "The body is both good and bad. We should rise superior to the body, and think of God. If we look at it from one point of view, the body is a storehouse of miseries, a mine of diseases, the birth-place of foulness, the unholy of unholies. From another point of view, the body is good and beautiful, the source of happiness, and a means of spiritual realisation. Yet, again, the body is merely a curdled product of menstrual blood, a net of desire and infatuation, and a prey to death. In another way, it is a pure thing, the treasure of treasures, the temple of God, the means for getting rid of worldly existence. We should give neither happiness nor unhappiness to the body. The body is neither good nor bad. We should rise superior to it, and think of God" (Abg. 4113). "He, who cares for the body," says Tukā, "cares for honour and repute, and thus becomes a prey to evil and suffering. . . . Consciousness of honour puts a stop to further progress, and enthrals a man by tying a rope round his neck" (Abg. 2537). Tukārāma advises the spiritual aspirant to look upon pleasure and pain alike. "He may be a carrier of water at one time, and sleep on a costly couch at another. He may now eat dainties, and now again he may have to eat bread without salt. At one time, he may go in a palanquin, and at another he may be obliged to go barefooted. Once, he may wear rich clothes, at another time, worn-out rags. . . . The spiritual aspirant," says Tukā, "should look upon pleasure and pain alike" (Abg. 2046). Tukārāma tells us not to tell a lie on any account whatsoever. "Even if a man were to help a marriage by telling a lie, he should not do it, because he would thereby merely go to hell. Dharma, the eldest of the

Pāṇḍavas, lost his thumb for having told a lie. A man who has a lie in his heart," says Tukā, "is bound to suffer" (Abg. 1021). He teaches that what is wanted is internal purity and not external purification. "Even if the body is purified outside, the mind is dirty inside. . . . It is full of untruth and hypocrisy. Be thou thy own spectator. Wear the sacred cloth in the shape of freedom from passion. Only then wilt thou be really pure" (Abg. 1551). "Holy waters do not cleanse the wickedness within. They cleanse only the external skin. The bitter Vṛindāvana fruit will not lose its bitterness even if it be put into sugar. There is no use sobbing unless you have tranquillity, forgiveness, and compassion" (Abg. 1131). "We should empty the heart of its contents, and then will God live in it. No other remedy is required," says Tukā, "to see God. We should nip all our desires in the bud. Where desires end, God comes to inhabit," says Tukā (Abg. 907). He tells us elsewhere that for reaching God, one is required to kill all one's desires. One need not look at a mark with concentration. One need not give anything in charity, or undergo penance. One need not forsake actions due to one's natural caste. One should only take leave of his desires, and then one would be able to realise God (Abg. 1405). In fact, if one meditates on God, Tukārāma allows him the enjoyment of all things whatsoever. "One need not leave food, nor go to a forest. One should meditate on God, and enjoy all things. A child sitting on the shoulder of its mother knows not the travail of walking. One need not consider what things to possess, and what things to abandon. One should only rest in God" (Abg. 816). Tukārāma does not even prevent a man from doing bad things, if by them one is able to reach God. One should not care for the preceptor's advice, if by that God may stand at a distance. . . . The wives of the ancient Ṛishis disobeyed their husbands, and went food in hand to Kṛishṇa. . . . Prahlāda made enmity with his father for the sake of God. . . . The wives of the cow-herds committed adultery with God. One should do even a bad deed," says Tukā, "provided by it he reaches God; and one should not do even a good deed by which God may stand at distance" (Abg. 680). "The spiritual aspirant must always live in the company of the

Saints, for other company may take away his mind from God. If one goes to see anybody at all, he should go to see a Saint. If one lives in the company of anybody, it should be in the company of the Saints. . . . The Saints are an ocean of happiness," says Tukā. "God is their treasure. They speak no other language but of God. One should find rest only in the Saints" (Abg. 712). "One should not wait for a suitable opportunity to turn up to meditate on God. One should begin immediately. One can never hope to be so unperturbed as to give oneself unmolested to mere meditation on God. If a man says that he will meditate on God when matters are comparatively easy, that will never come to pass" (Abg. 1181). "Whatever be the difficulties in which one may be placed, one should offer prayers to God. One should call in the help of God, when calamities befall him. Then God will not wait, but ward off those calamities by his personal intervention. By meditation on God's name, obstacles will vanish away in different directions. One need only surrender his life to God" (Abg. 1625). "Thus God should be the sole object of the aspirant's meditation, even in dreams and in sleep.

His mind should know no other object of contemplation. The natural bent of the senses should be in the direction of God, and the eyes should ever seek His vision" (Abg. 318).

VI. THE TEACHER AND THE DISCIPLE

The Teacher and the Disciple

52. In the opinion of Tukārāma, he alone deserves to be a Spiritual Teacher, who regards his disciples as gods. "He, who does not accept service from his disciples and regards them as gods, is alone worthy of being a Teacher. . . . In him alone does knowledge live, because he is indifferent to self. I tell the truth," says Tukā, "and care not for people who may become angry with me for saying so" (Abg. 881). "A spiritual teacher must not fatten his body. Unless the true mark of Sainthood has been generated in him, he is not worthy of making disciples. He who cannot swim himself should not make others catch hold of him in the waters. . . . If an exhausted man goes to another exhausted man, both of them will perish," says Tukā (Abg. 3122). "A false teacher makes his disciples look uninterruptedly at a mark, and tells them to see the light by rubbing their eyes. He falsely teaches his disciples that he has thus enjoyed Samādhi, and deceives them. . . . He earns his livelihood by teaching any falsehood he pleases. . . . He teaches his disciples to utter the name of the Guru himself" (Abg. 3431). "His disciples, on the other hand, go from bad to worse, and take no account of castes. They regard a holy man as a thorn in their way, and regard the pariah as a very spiritual man. . . . This Guru gives spiritual advice to concubines, children, and some foolish Brahmins. . . . They all eat together, and say that such inter-dining takes them to absolution. Such Gurus and disciples both go to hell," says Tukā (Abg. 3432). "A true Guru therefore should not be merely worthy of his instruction, but should see that his disciples are also worthy of his instruction. One should never force one's spiritual advice upon others. Does not a juggler keep a monkey with him? . . . He, who wastes seed in a place which is not wet with water, is a fool. I distribute spiritual advice like rain," says Tukā (Abg. 1714).

VII. THE NAME

The Celebration of God's Name as the Way to Realisation

53. The sole way to the realisation of God, according to Tukārāma, is the constant repetition of God's name. "Sit silent," says Tukārāma, "compose thy mind and make it pure, and then happiness will know no bounds. God will certainly come and dwell in his heart. This will be the result of thy long effort. Meditate time after time on God's name,—Rāma, Kṛishṇa, Hari. I declare," says Tukā, "that this will surely come to pass, if thou hast one-pointed devotion" (Abg. 1132). "The uttering of the name of God is indeed an easy way for reaching Him. One need not go to a distant forest. God will Himself come to the house of a Saint. One should sit at a place, concentrate his mind, invoke God with love, and utter His name time after time. I swear by God's name," says Tukā, "that there is no other way for reaching God: indeed, this is the easiest of all ways" (Abg. 1698). "If we only utter the name of God, God will stand before us. In that way should we meditate on Him. He, who does not present Himself to the vision of the gods, dances when His devotee sings" (Abg. 2021). There are always difficulties which intervene before God is reached. These are dispelled by the power of devotion. "The Name will lead to God if no obstacle intervenes. A fruit becomes ripe on a tree only if it is not plucked" (Abg. 695). "The ship of God's name," says Tukā, "will ultimately carry one across the ocean of life. It will save both the young and the old" (Abg. 2457). "All the different Sciences proclaim the supremacy of the Name. The Vedas tell us that nothing but the Name of God shall save us. The different Śāstras say the same thing. Throughout the different Purāṇas," says Tukā, "the same message is preached" (Abg. 3128). He alone who knows the efficacy of the Name, says Tukā, may be said to have grasped the inner meaning of the Vedas. "We alone know the real meaning of the Vedas; others merely bear the burden of knowing. The man who sees is not the man who tastes. The man who bears the burden is not he who owns the burden. The secret of the creation, preservation, and destruction of the world is with God. We have found out the root," says Tukā. "The fruit will now come of itself to hand" (Abg. 1549). There are some occasions when one does not know what one's duty is. In such a case, says Tukārāma, we should utter the name of God. "We do not know what to do, and what not to do: we only know how to meditate on Thy feet. . . . We do not know where to go, and where not to go: we only know how to meditate on Thy name. By Thy making," says Tukā, "sins become merits. By our making," says Tukā, "merits become sins" (Abg. 3307). "Thus determinately and resolutely should one meditate on God by means of His Name. Let the head break off, or let the body fall, we should not leave off the celebration of God's Name. Even if we are fasting for a week, we should not fail to sing the Name of God. If the head breaks, or the body is cut in twain, we should not fail in the celebration of God's Name. He alone, who determinately utters the Name of God," says Tukā, "will be able to find God" (Abg. 3258).

Bodily and Mental Effects of Meditation on the Name

54. Tukārāma next goes on to discuss the physical and mental effects of meditation on the Name. "When I utter Thy name, my mind becomes composed. The tongue enjoys a stream of ambrosia. Good omens of all kinds take place. The mind is coloured in Thy vision, and becomes steady on Thy feet. . . . One becomes as satisfied as if one has taken a dainty meal. Desires come to an end, and words come out of the mouth as of complete satisfaction. Happiness meets happiness, and there is no limit to blessedness" (Abg. 830). Tukārāma repeats the same idea elsewhere. "The whole body feels cool when one meditates on the Name. The senses forget their movements. . . . By the sweet nectar-like love of God, one is full of energy and all kinds of sorrow depart immediately" (Abg. 1543). "The body which was hitherto unclean, becomes lustrous by the power of the Name, the mind is purified, and repentance puts a stop to one's accumulated Karma" (Abg. 3997). " . . . The evil passions are conquered; all the impulses are nipped in the bud by the power of the Name. Tukā looks at God's feet, and waits for His answer" (Abg. 3302).

The Moral Effects of Meditation on the Name

55. The moral effects of uttering the Name, Tukārāma is never wearied of describing. The utterance of the Name, he tells us, brings with it exceeding merit. "He who utters the name of God while walking, gets the merit of a Sacrifice at every step. Blessed is his body. It is itself a place of pilgrimage. He who says God while doing his work, is always merged in Samādhi. He who utters the name of God while eating, gets the merit of a fast even though he may have taken his meals. He who utters the name of God without intermission receives liberation though living" (Abg. 3667). "Even if one were to give in charity the whole earth encircled by the seas, that cannot equal the merit of uttering the Name. . . . A repetition of all the Vedas cannot equal one Name of God. All places of pilgrimage have no value before God's Name. All sorts of bodily toils are useless before the Name of God" (Abg.

1581). "By the power of the Name of God, one shall come to know what one does not know. One shall see what cannot be seen. One will be able to speak what cannot be spoken. One shall meet what cannot be ordinarily met. Incalculable will be the gain of uttering the Name," says Tukā (Abg. 2220). Yet, again, Tukārāma says in another place: "Untold benefits will accrue if we sing the Name of God in solitude. We should pacify our desires, and should not give room to any passions. We should not waste words, but should utter the Name, which is as the arrow which will hit the mark" (Abg. 1093). The Name of God, says Tukārāma, will save us from all difficulties. "Enclose the Name of God in your mouth. Think constantly of what is valuable and what is not valuable. By meditation on God, all difficulties will vanish. We shall thus be able to cross the uncrossable ocean of life. . . . The whole lineage will become pure," says Tukā, "by the utterance of God's Name" (Abg. 3137). The medicine of God's name, we are told elsewhere, destroys the disease of life. "Drink the medicine of God's Name, and all your agonies will cease. Partake of nothing but the name of God. Even the disease of life will thus vanish, not to speak of other small diseases" (Abg. 1384). Tukārāma tells us elsewhere that in this perishable life, the only rest is in the name of God. "The body is subject to all kinds of accidents, good and bad. Its happiness and sorrow are both evenescent. The only thing to be achieved in this life is love towards God. . . . The only rest," says Tukā, "in this mortal existence is in the constant remembrance of God's Name" (Abg. 1859). One will even be able to confer spiritual obligations upon others by uttering God's Name. "One should not flutter about, but should remain steady, believing in the efficacy of God's Name. God will give you imperishable happiness, and the round of incarnations will cease. You will even be able to confer obligations upon others. That itself will be a great asset. The Name of God will save you in this life as well as in the next. If you leave off the pursuit of evanescent things," says Tukā, "you will attain to incalculable bliss" (Abg. 670). "The sweetness of the Name is indescribable. The tongue soon gets averse to other kinds of flavours; but the flavour of the Name increases every moment. Other medicines lead you to death; but this medicine relieves you of death. God has become our constant food," says Tukā (Abg. 1168). Tukārāma is so completely satisfied with the utterance of the Name that he is not desirous of anything else. He tells God that he has no desire for anything except His name. All kinds of powers which may accrue in contemplation are useless before the power of devotion. Tukā says that, by the power of the Name, he will easily go to heaven, and will enjoy complete bliss (Abg. 231). Finally, the sweetness of God's Name, Tukārāma tells us, cannot be known by God Himself. "Does a lotus plant know the fragrance of its flowers? It is the bee which tastes of its fragrance. The cow eats grass; but the calf alone know the sweetness of her milk. The oyster shell cannot enjoy its own pearls; similarly," says Tukā, "God does not know the sweetness of the Name, which only the devotees can experience" (Abg. 233).

VIII. THE KĪRTANA

Kīrtana, as a Way of Realising God

56. There is another way to the realisation of God—one closely related to the celebration of the Name. It is what may be called the "Kīrtana," or the singing of the praises of God, either in the abstract, or in His concrete manifestations in human life. Tukārāma was given to the celebration of the Kīrtana like many other Saints. "The Kīrtana," says Tukā, "is the meditation of God Himself. . . . There is no merit on earth which is equal to that of the Kīrtana. Believe me," says Tukā, "God stands up where Kīrtana is being performed. . . . A man who performs the Kīrtana not only saves himself, but also others. Without doubt," says Tukā, "one can meet God by performing a Kīrtana" (Abg. 1604). Hence, anybody who disbelieves in the Kīrtana merely ruins himself. "The words of one who does not believe in the Kīrtana of God are unwholesome; his ears are like a rat's hole. Vainly do such people leave away sacred nectar, and follow after insignificant things. Vainly do people go astray, and become mad in their endeavour," says Tukā (Abg. 3381). "He alone attends a Kīrtana who wishes to uplift himself. Nobody asks an ant to go where sugar is to be found. A beggar seeks out a donor of his own accord. He who is hungry goes and finds out food. He who suffers from a disease, goes of his own accord to the house of a doctor. He who wishes to uplift himself," says Tukā, "never fails to attend a Kīrtana" (Abg. 1620). Tukārāma only prays that his body may be kept sound, in order that it might help him in the singing of God's praise. "A Kīrtana requires soundness of limbs. Do not allow my limbs to grow weak, O God. I do not mind if my life is cut short. But so long as I live, let me be sound," says Tukā, "in order that I may pray to Thee" (Abg. 4023).

Kīrtana is a River Which Flows Upward Towards God

57. Tukārāma often likens Kīrtana to a river. In one place, he tells us that it is a river which flows upwards towards God. "The Kīrtana is a stream of nectar flowing before God. It wends upwards, and is the crown of all holy things. It is the life-blood of Śiva and burns up all kinds of sins. The gods themselves describe its power," says Tukā (Abg. 3382). In another place, he describes Kīrtana as a confluence of three rivers. "It is a confluence where God and Devotee and the Name meet together. The very sands at the place are holy. Mountains of sins are burnt by its power. It spreads holiness among all men and women. Holy places come to it to be purified. It is more sacred than the sacred days. Its holiness is incomparable, and the gods themselves are unable to describe the happiness produced by it" (Abg. 1605).

Requirements of a Man Who Performs Kīrtana

58. What, according to Tukārāma, are the requirements of a man who performs a Kīrtana? "If I were to perform a Kīrtana by accepting money for it, let, O God, my body be destroyed. If I were to request anybody to arrange for my Kīrtana, let, O God, my tongue fall down. Thou art our helper, and there is nothing lacking before Thee. Why should I waste my words before others? At Thy feet are all powers, and Thou art my

Lord" (Abg. 3138). "Where one performs a Kīrtana, one should not take food. One should not have his forehead besmeared with fragrant scent. One should not allow himself to be garlanded by flowers. One should not ask for grain or for grass for a horse or a bullock. They who give money, and they who accept money," says Tukā, "both of them go to hell" (Abg. 2256). In this way, Tukārāma tells us that pecuniary bargains are an obstacle to spiritual progress.

Great is the Power of Song

59. Tukārāma tells us very often that the power imparted by a Kīrtana is indescribable. "Great is the power of Song," says Tukā. "This evidently is Thy grace. Allow me to consecrate my life to Thy service. Let my mind be so filled by Thy love that there may be neither any ebb nor any flow to it. Let my words be a mine of sweet nectar," says Tukā (Abg. 309). He elsewhere tells us that the joy of Kīrtana is indescribable. "The Saints have told us an easy secret: they have asked us to dance with Tāla and Diṇḍī in our hands. The happiness of ecstasy is as nothing before this happiness of a Kīrtana. It continually grows, and one is merged in it by the power of his devotion. No doubts now harass his mind, the mind becomes tranquil, and all kinds of misery vanish immediately" (Abg. 766). Tukārāma tells us that there is no entrance for the Messengers of death where a Kīrtana is being performed. "Death tells his messengers—Go not to the place where the Name is being celebrated. You have not power over that place. You do not go to the place where the Name-bearers live. Go not even to its outskirts. The great disc of God moves round and wards off all dangers. God Himself stands as a door-keeper at the place with a bludgeon and the moving disc in His hands. . . . The Saints are the most powerful beings on earth—so says Death to his servants" (Abg. 1608). While a Kīrtana is beng performed, nothing can cause fear to the Saints. "God is before, and behind. Why need the Saints fear anything at all? Dance with the power of joy, and allow not your mind to be tossed by doubts. How can Death come and have power before God? When the all-powerful God is present, what can be lacking to the Saints?" (Abg. 350). Tukārāma tells us that he is always beating the cymbals, and dancing in joy for God. He has been telling people that there is really no fearbefore God. He has been singing and dancing in tune with Ṭāḷas and Bells. Fear can do nothing to us," says Tukā, "for God comes before us" (Abg. 357). Finally, we are told that the merit of Kīrtana is superior to the merit of any penance, or the counting of beads. "For, in Kīrtana," says Tukārāma, "God is verily present. Believe thee words of mine,and allow not your mind to wander. All ecstasy and all penance live," says Tukā, "by the power of Kīrtana" (Abg. 2142).

IX. BHAKTI

God Cannot Be Reached Except Through Love

60. Generally speaking, meditation on the Name, or performance of a Kīrtana, are merely external marks of an internal devotion or Bhakti. Tukārāma tells us that when a man has this Bhakti, he may be said to have performed all religious functions whatsoever. "When a man has placed his mind, and words, and body at Thy service, there is no duty for him which he need perform. Why need he worship any stones? . . . Why need he bathe in the holy waters? What sins can he be relieved thereby? I have submitted all my desires to Thee, and have conquered all sin and merit. . . .When the body has been made over to Thee, one need only rest silent in contentment" (Abg. 1183). "In this way, the Bhaktimārga," says Tukā, "is the only easy pathway in this age. All other ways have been useless. God Viṭṭhala stands up, raises his arm, and calls his servants to duty. Those who believe in Him will cross the ocean of life. Others, who do not believe, shall go to ruin" (Abg. 1582). Tukārāma tells us also that the transpersonal God cannot be reached except through love."God has no form, nor any name, nor any place, where He can be seen; but wherever you go, you see God. He has neither form nor transformation; but He fills the whole world. He is neither impersonal nor personal; but is beyond all knowledge. This God," says "Tukā, cannot be attained except through love" (Abg. 2148). In fact, God does not care for anything except love. He does not care for a sweet voice: he only looks to the heart within. "If God has not given us a sweet voice and if we cannot speak sweetly, let us not be afraid. God does not care for these attainments. Say Rāma, Kṛishṇa, Hari as you can. Demand of God a pure love for Him, and a belief in Him" (Abg. 7). "One need not worship stones, or brass, or any kind of images. What is required is pure devotion. That is the way to liberation. What is the use of these rosaries, and these garlands? Why need we care for a learned voice? Why need we care for a beautiful song? If we have no devotion, God will not care for us," says Tukā (Abg. 2054). Let a man believe fully, and he will be saved by God. "He who attempts to know God at the cost of his life shall be saved by God. There is no doubt that he will reach the other side of existence. Blessed is he who believes; for in him alone God lives. God becomes the bond-servant of those," says Tukā, "who blindly believe in Him" (Abg. 4028). Absence of real devotion makes God stand away from those who entertain doubt and fear. . . . God stands away from those who cannot sacrifice their life for God. God stands away from those who speak vain words without any real sacrifice. God knows the hearts of all, and will reward them as they deserve" (Abg. 3874).

Images to Describe the Relation of Devotee to God

61. Tukārāma employs various images to describe the devotee's love for God. In one place, he tells us that a devotee should throw himself on God, as a Satī on her husband. "When a Satī sees the cremation fire of her husband, her hair stands on end in joy. . . . She does not look at her family, and her wealth. She does not weep. She only remembers her husband, and throws herself in the funeral pyre" (Abg. 1245). Even so must a devotee throw himself in God. In another place, he says, we should fall straight into Brahman, as a fly flies into a flame. "If we want to enjoy God, we should lop off our head from our body, and hold it in our hands. We should set all our belongings on fire, and should not look behind. We should be as bold," says Tukā, "as a fly, which falls straight into a flame" (Abg.

3414). In a third place, he tells us that the devotee's spirit should rise to God like a fountain. "As a fountain rises upwards, even so must one's spirit rise to God. One should entertain no idea whatsoever, except that of God" (Abg. 801). Only then would we be able to reach God. Fourthly, he tells us that we should as much love to hear of God's praises, as a mother of her son's exploits. "As a mother is delighted to hear the good news of her son, even so must our mind be delighted to hear of God's praise. We must forget bodily consciousness like a deer which is infatuated by music. We must look up to God, as the young ones of a tortoise look up to their mother" (Abg. 3426). In fact, the mind that is engrossed in God should think only of God, and of nothing else. "One should know, and yet know not, being merged in the love of God. One should live in this life uncontaminated by it, as a lotus-leaf lives in water uncontaminated by its drops. Praise and censure must fall on his ears as if he were engaged in a state of ecstasy. One should see the world and yet not see it, as if he were in a dream. Unless this happens," says Tukā, "whatever a man may do is of no avail" (Abg. 2179).

X. CASTES

Caste Not Recognised in God-devotion

62. Tukārāma teaches us that the castes have no significance for God-realisation. A man may belong to any caste whatsoever. If he only devotes himself to the service of God, he will be regarded as holy. "Holy is the family, and holy the country where the servants of God are born. They have devoted, and by them all the three worlds become holy. Pride of caste has never made any man holy," says Tukā. "The untouchables have crossed the ocean of life by God-devotion, and the Purāṇas sing their praises. . . . Gorā, the potter, Rohidāsa, the shoe-maker, Kabīra, the Muslim, Senā, the barber, Kanhopātrā, the concubine, . . . Chokhāmeḷā, the outcast . . . Janābāī, the maid . . . have all become unified with God by their devotion. The Vedas and the Śāstras have said that for the service of God, castes do not matter. Inquire into the various works," says Tukā, "and you will find that unholy men become holy by God-devotion" (Abg. 3241). "Musk looks ugly," says Tukā, "but its essence is wonderful. The sandal trees present no good appearance, but their fragrance spreads all round. A Parisa is ugly to look at, but it creates gold. A sword when melted does not bring a pie; but by its own quality, it sells for a thousand coins. Castes do not matter," says Tukā, "it is God's Name that matters" (Abg. 2194). "The cow eats all kinds of dung; but it is yet holy. The brooks that enter into a river become identified with it. The holy Pippala is born of the crow's excreta. The family of the Pāndavas was not a holy one. . . . Ajāmela, Kubjā and Vidura were not born of a high caste. Vālhā, Viśvāmitra, Vaśishṭha and Nārada cannot boast of a high lineage. Whatever unholy deeds are commited by men and women, when they remember God with repentance, they become free from sins" (Abg. 122). "A Brahmin who does not like the Name of God, is not a Brahmin. I tell you," says Tukā, "that when he was born, his mother had committed adultery with a Mahāra. . . . " (Abg. 706).

"An outcast who loves the Name of God is verily a Brahmin. In him have tranquillity and forbearance, compassion and courage, made their home. When all the different passions have left a man's mind, he is as good as a Brahmin," says Tukā (Abg. 707). Even though Tukārāma generally holds such opinions, he elsewhere respects a Brahmin because he is born a Brahmin. "Even if a she-ass gives milk, will she be equal to a cow? Even if a crow's neck is decorated by flowers, can it equal a swan? Even if a monkey bathes and puts a Tilaka on its forehead, can it equal a Brahmin? A Brahmin," says Tukā, "even though he is fallen from his high station, must yet be respected" (Abg. 2223). Finally, Tukārāma tells us that we must recognise the difference of castes while we are living in this world. The difference, says Tukārāma, vanishes only in the ecstatic state. "I tell you, O Saints, that the different castes have been born of the same Being according to their merits and demerits. . . . The mango tree, the jujube tree, the fig tree, and the sandal tree are different so long as they are not reduced to cinders in the same fire. The difference of castes must be taken into account," says Tukā, "until it vanishes in the ecstatic state" (Abg. 920).

XI. THE GOD OF PAṆḌHARAPŪR

Description of the God of Paṇḍharapūr

63. It cannot be gainsaid that Tukārāma for a long while looked upon Viṭṭhala, the God of Paṇḍharapūr, as the cynosure of his eyes. It was only later that he began to find that God was everywhere. Tukārāma, however, always tried to place before the mind's eye of the people some concrete object for worship, and this he succeeded in doing by calling them to the worship of Viṭṭhala. "My heart pants," he says, "for seeing the face of the God of Paṇḍarapūr. The God who stands on a brick at Paṇḍharapūr with his beautiful form, has ravished my heart. My eyes can never be too much satisfied by looking at Him. My life-breath seems to take leave of my body if I am unable for a while to see the beautiful face of God. My mind has been ravished," says Tukā, "by the son of Nanda, who has the Eagle for His banner" (Abg. 1700). Tukārāma tells us that neither any wealth nor any happiness pleases him. His mind is always set after going to Paṇḍharapūr. When shall the 11th day of Āshāḍha dawn, he asks, so that he may be able to go to Pandharī? It is only when a man is anxious to see God, says Tukā, that God is anxious to meet him (Abg. 1600). "The Saints have planted aloft the banner of God. I look at that banner as His ensign, and lose myself in His name. If you go by the path indicated by the banner of God, you will surely be able to find God" (Abg. 2871). "This is verily the pathway by which the Saints of old have gone. Mythologies tell us that we must not go by unbeaten paths. The way to God is so bright and straight, that nobody need ask any other man about it. Banners are flying aloft, and the eagle ensign is shining in the air," says Tukā (Abg. 188). Hitherto many have walked by the way which leads to Paṇḍharapūr. "We have heard of many people who have harboured the Name of God in their minds. They have crossed the ocean of life, and have gone to the other shore. Let us go by the very same way as much as may lie within our power. The ferry which has carried them has been reserved for us, and there shall now be no delay. We need not pay even a farthing for it. We need only have devotion. The ferry is on the banks of the Bhīmā. Let us swim by it to where God is waiting and standing straight to receive us" (Abg. 2683). "The ferry is now on the banks of the Chandrabhāgā. Take away the infinite booty of God's wealth, O Saints! The banner of God's Name is flying aloft. Tukārāma is a porter on the ferry, but God carries his load" (Abg. 993). "When we reach the other shore of the Chandrabhāgā, God is standing there to exchange love for weariness. The poverty and hunger of the people shall disappear. The most generous of gods, the God of Pandharī, raises His arm, and makes you a sign to approach. He shall embrace the ignorant more than the wise. . . . We are the helpless, we are the poor in spirit," says Tukā, "and God will protect us" (Abg. 1427). When we go to the temple of Paṇḍharī, the image disappears, and infinite light takes its place. The God of Paṇḍharī is merely the external symbol of an all-immanent light. "The light within, which had remained hitherto hidden, will now begin to appear. The whole universe cannot contain the bliss of the moment. What happiness can be compared to it? The God, who is standing on the brick, is an external symbol of our devotion, though he is Himself impersonal," says Tukā (Abg. 2069). "The God of Paṇḍharī is a manifestation of Kṛishṇa, who as a child lived in the house of Nanda, and who could show the whole universe within Himself. Him who gave satisfaction to the whole world, Yaśodā was trying to feed. Him who filled the whole universe, the cow-herd women were taking on their lap. Verily of various wiles is this God, says Tukā, Who keeps His celibacy intact in spite of His enjoyment" (Abg. 3747). "God Viṭṭhala indeed is a great thief. He has taken the net of devotion in His hands, and has come to Paṇḍharī. He has deceived the whole world, and does not allow Himself to be seen. He raises His hand, and ensnares the eyes of those who wish to see Him. This thief has been brought by Puṇḍalīka to Paṇḍharī. Let us go," says Tukā, "and catch hold of Him" (Abg. 442). Puṇḍalīka himself, says

Tukārāma, has become arrogant by the power of his devotion, and has made Viṭṭhala stand up. "Thou hast become arrogant by the love of Viṭṭhala, O Puṇḍalīka! How audacious that you throw away a brick, and make Viṭṭhala stand on it. God is standing there for such a length of time, and yet you do not ask Him to sit down" (Abg. 2965). "The ghost of Paṇḍharī," says Tukārāma, "is indeed a powerful ghost, and possesses everybody who goes that way. Verily full of goblins is this forest, and the mind becomes possessed when it goes there. Go not there," says Tukā, "for those who go there do not return. Tukā went to Paṇḍarī and never came back to life" (Abg. 3115). One need not aspire after going to heaven: one need only go to Paṇḍharapūr, says Tukārāma. "Go to Paṇḍharī, and become a Vārakarī. Why dost thou aspire after heaven, if thou goest to the sand-banks of Paṇḍharapūr? Tukārāma falls prostrate before the Saints who bear the banner of God on their shoulders, put on garlands of the Tulasī plant on their necks, and besmear their foreheads by the sweet scent that is sacred to God" (Abg. 2248).

XII. TUKĀRĀMA'S THEISM

The Personal Superior to the Impersonal

64. It is an easy passage from the worship of God in this manner to a theistic view of the God-head which does not allow formlessness to the object of worship. Tukārāma tells us often that he would not allow God to be formless. "Be formless as others desire; but for me take Thou on a form, O God! . . . I have fallen in love with Thy name. Do not suffer my devotion to wane. Thou mayest hold out for me the bait of liberation: but go and deceive the philosophers by that bait. I tell Thee that Thou shouldst not allow the stream of my devotion to grow dry" (Abg. 2410). "We have slighted liberation for this sake, and are content to re-incarnate again and again. The nectar of devotion only increases our desire from day to day. We have made God to take on a form, and shall not allow Him to become Impersonal" (Abg. 1116). Tukārāma tells us that God is obliged to take on a form in fear of His devotees. "A bee can pierce a hard tree; but it is enclosed by a little flower. Love is bound by love, and is encased in its bonds. A little child makes even an elderly parent powerless by its love. God," says Tukā, "is obliged to take on a form in fear of His devotee" (Abg. 1282).

He Who Says He Has Become God is a Fool

65. As Tukārāma does not allow God to become formless, so he does not allow man, howsoever high and magnanimous he may be, to identify himself with God. "Thou shouldst be my Lord, and I Thy servant. Thy place should be high, and my place low. . . . Water does not swallow water. A tree does not swallow its fruits. A diamond appears beautiful on account of its setting. Gold looks beautiful when it is transformed into ornaments. . . . Shade gives pleasure when there is the Sun outside. A mother gives out milk when there is a child to partake of it. What happiness can there be when one meets oneself? I am happy," says Tukā, "in the belief that I am not liberated" (Abg. 595). And thus he, who calls himself God, is a fool. "Some say that they have become gods; but these will surely go to hell. God has lifted up the earth: a man cannot lift even a bag of rice. God has killed great demons: a man cannot cut even a piece of straw. He who aspires to the throne of God," says Tukā, "hides a mine of sins" (Abg. 3274). He who says that he has seen God is also a fool. "He is the greatest of rogues who says that he has seen God. How can the bonds of existence be unloosed by the advice of such a man? He drowns himself as well as others. There is no fool on this earth," says Tukā, "comparable to him, who calls himself God" (Abg. 2064).

Service of God's Feet Superior to an Advaitic Identification with God

66. Tukārāma prizes the service of the feet of God more than an Advaitic identification with Him. "Advaitism pleases me not" says Tukā. "Give me the service of Thy feet. . . . Reserve for me the relation between God and devotee, and fill me with happiness" (Abg. 2884). He tells us also that he does not want Self-knowledge. He only wishes to be God's devotee, and talk with Him. "I do not want Self-knowledge. Make me a devotee of Thine, O God! Show me Thy form, and let me place my head on Thy feet. I shall look at Thee, shall embrace Thee, and shall sacrifice my body for Thee. When

Thou askest, I shall speak with Thee good things in solitude" (Abg. 3308). Tukārāma repeats the idea elsewhere also. "I do not want Self-identity," he says, "I want the service of Thy feet. Let me be Thy servant from life to life. . . . What value has Liberation for me which does not sustain the sweet relation between God and Saint? How shall the Impersonal please me, as I cannot see His face?" (Abg. 2709). Even Videhamukti Tukārāma identifies with the service of the Lord. "We shall always sing the Name of God, and keep our mind content. We dance with joy, and have no idea even of our own existence. We enjoy the Videha state even during life. We are verily made of fire," says Tukā, "and shall dispel sin and merit alike" (Abg. 3229).

Rebirth Superior to Absolution

67. As Tukārāma supposes that the service of God is superior to unification with Him, so he also supposes that reincarnation is superior to the state of liberation. "Hear my prayer, O God. I do not want absolution. For, the happiness that springs from devotion is superior to the happiness that can spring from absolution. . . . The happiness of heaven has an end; but the happiness of the Name is infinite. Thou canst not know the greatness of Thy Name, says Tukā; hence it is that Thy devotees long for re-incarnation" (Abg. 910). "Let me safely incarnate," says Tukārāma elsewhere, "if I can constantly sing the praises of God, and if I can always live in the company of the Good. Then shall I not mind the trouble involved in re-incarnation time after time" (Abg. 1589). Re-incarnation is also desirable, says Tukā, if one can become a Vārakarī. "I shall take on a new birth," says Tukārāma, "if I can become a Vārakarī of Paṇḍharī. This is what I have personally experienced. Hence it is that I have sacrificed all other things for Thy sake" (Abg. 1652).

The Omnipotence of God

68. In fact, says Tukārāma, all things depend on God. With His great power, what can He not do? God indeed is the universal mover. He moves the body as well as the universe. "Who makes this body move? Who can make us speak except God Himself? It is God only who can make us hear or see. . . . He alone can continue the mind in its egoism. He it is who can make even the leaf of a tree move. . . . God has filled the Whole inside and outside. What can be lacking to Him in His universal presence?" (Abg. 3038). Man's business is only to rest in God, and to carry on his work without asking anything from Him. "Let the body be delivered over to God, and God will do as He pleases. He is the support of the whole world, and will bring about the proper thing at the proper moment. In this faith should we grow strong," says Tukā (Abg. 2229). "We should have no other belief except this. God is all-powerful, and can achieve anything whatsoever. Why need a man care for anything at all? He who pervades the universe, and directs the will,—what can He not accomplish? (Abg. 1174). What little power Tukārāma has, he says, is due to God. When the Saints had praised him for having possessed power, Tukārāma said that it was not his power, but God's. "Why do you burden me, O Saints, by attributing power to me? The doll cannot act in the absence of the puller. Could the monkeys have made the stones swim on the ocean in the absence of God? It is God who is the only mover. Everything else is inanimate in comparison, and God only uses it for His purposes" (Abg. 2057).

God Favours People According to Their Deserts

69. If God is omnipotent, man need ask whatever he desires of God alone. What is lacking to God, asks Tukārāma, that a man should beg of another? "In God, nothing is lacking, and the wandering beggar moves like a dog from door to door. He recites one passage after another only in order to gain a farthing. He praises some and censures others, and is full of anxiety at heart. The only fate which such a man deserves," says Tukārāma, "is that his face should be burnt in fire" (Abg. 1391). "Let us therefore ask whatever we desire of God alone. What is lacking to Him, whom all Powers serve? We must sacrifice our mind and body and speech to God. He who supports the whole universe cannot help supporting us" (Abg. 1392). Only, God favours people according to their deserts. "Rain pours down of its own accord; but the earth brings forth fruit according to its quality. Like seed, like crop. . . . To a lamp, the master of the house and the thief are both alike. A crow feeds upon a bullock's bone; the Tittira bird feeds upon pebbles; while the swan feeds upon pearls. . . . God indeed favours people according to their deserts" (Abg. 1320). "Nobody can withstand the will of God. King Hariśchandra and his wife Tārā served as drawers of water in the house of a pariah. The Pāndavas, who were the beloved of God, were dethroned from their place. Our business is merely to sit silent, and watch the progress of events" (Abg. 1031). And when it is said that God favours people according to their deserts, it follows that we must cultivate goodness and avoid evil. To Tukārāma, evil has a reality in this world. "The fire may serve to ward off cold; but you cannot gather it in the hem of your garment. Scorpions and serpents may indeed be God; but we must respect them at a distance, and not touch them" (Abg. 637). "From the same curds come out both butter and butter-milk; but the two cannot be priced at the same value. On the sky appear both the moon and the stars; but both are not of equal lustre.

From the same earth come pebbles and diamonds; but the two cannot be priced equally. Similarly," says Tukā, "Saints and Sinners are both men; but we cannot worship the two alike" (Abg. 1730).

XIII. GOD'S OFFICE FOR THE SAINTS

God's Office for the Saints

70. God has a particular fascination for His Saints. They have made God the all-in-all of their life. True servants as they are, they are not be afraid of their Master. "Why need a true servant be afraid of his master? In arguing with his master, a true servant feels greater and greater delight. When one feels that he is in the right, he need not be afraid of anybody" (Abg. 283). Moreover, a true Saint has dedicated all his powers to God. "Whatever powers there may be with us, we shall place them at the service of the Lord. We have delivered over our life to God, and have wiped off considerations of life and death. What now remains is God only. He it is who eats, He it is who speaks, He it is who sings, and He it is who dances," says Tukā (Abg. 795). "Shall not God who supports the whole world give support to a Saint in time of need? Why need not a Saint rest content in the belief that God will support him? Why should he not remember the kindness of the Lord who caters for the whole world, who creates milk in the mother's breasts for the child and makes the two grow together? Trees put forth new foliage in summer. Tell me now who waters them? . . . Remember Him who is called the All-supporting, for He will certainly support thee" (Abg. 1593). " . . . In the bosom of a stone there is a frog. Who feeds this frog but God? The birds and the serpents do not lay by anything. Who finds food for them except God? When thou hast thrown all thy burden on God, Ocean of Compassion as He is, He shall not neglect thee" (Abg. 290). In this sure belief of the power of the all-supporting God, we should rest content and not beg before men. For begging before men means disbelief in God. "Shame to the man who takes the begging bowl in his hand. God should neglect such a fellow. He has no devotion for God in his heart, and shows merely a devotional exterior. Not to deliver over one's life to God is to commit adultery with Him. What a great misfortune and what a great disbelief in God, that in poverty of spirit a man should throw his burden upon the world!" (Abg. 858). God does not indeed neglect a devotee who is prepared to go to the uttermost extreme of penance for him. "One should throw away all sense of shame, and invoke God by the power of one's devotion. One should catch hold of trees, partake of their leaves, and invoke God. One should sew together rags of cloth, cover one's loins with them, and invoke the grace of God. A man who goes to this length in seeking God shall never be neglected by Him" (Abg. 1729). "He who follows God, shall never be left by Him in the lurch. Near his body and near his mind, God stands as an eternal witness, and gives him as he deserves" (Abg. 3910). "And devotees wait upon God only because they firmly believe that no devotee can come to naught. They raise their hands and invoke God to come to their help. . . . " (Abg. 1073). "And God does really come to their rescue. What is, however, wanted is patience. God shall never leave His Saints uncared-for. Sing, O Saints, in joy," says Tukā. "God's great power will turn away the predations of Death. Is not the mother prepared to go to the uttermost extreme in saving her child when it is attacked with a disease? God indeed is greater than the mother. I have personally experienced," says Tukā, "that true devotion is ever crowned with success" (Abg. 665). Occasionally, God takes pleasure in throwing His devotees in the midst of difficulties. "God is very cruel," says Tukā. "He has no affection and mercy. . . . He deprived Hariś-chandra of his kingdom, . . . separated Nala and Damayantī, . . . tried King Śibi's generosity, . . . asked Karṇa for charity at a critical occasion, . . . deprived Bali of all his wealth, . . . and made Śriyāḷa kill his own son. Those who devotedly worship Thee, O God, Thou compellest to renounce all pleasure in life" (Abg. 105). "But, ultimately, God does ward off all evil from His Saints. He comes to their rescue all of a sudden. He seems to be nowhere, and yet comes all at once. He reserves happiness for His devotees, and takes for Himself their lot of sorrow" (Abg. 264). "His devotees need not, therefore, entertain any fear or anxiety. . . . They should only maintain courage, bear courageously the buffets of fortune, and God will show Himself near them, . . . because, in fact, He fills the whole world" (Abg. 328). "When Death is before and behind, one should not run, for one's efforts will be of no avail. One should only invoke God, and God will come and take His devotee on His shoulders" (Abg. 781). "For, who shall kill him whom God saves? Such a one may wander bare-footed in the whole forest, and yet not a single thorn may pierce his feet. He cannot be drowned in water. He cannot be killed by poison. He can never fall into the clutches of Death. When bullets and missiles are hurled at him, God will protect him" (Abg. 1017). "And God will attend upon His devotee with all happiness. It is the duty of His devotee to remember Him at every step, and then God will follow him with all happiness. He will hold His beautiful cloth as a cover to protect him from the sun" (Abg. 1048). "God has warded off the pecuniary difficulties of His Saints. He has helped Kabīra and Nāmadeva and

Ekanātha" (Abg. 67). "When His devotees have sat in caverns, He has been their attendant. He has warded off their hunger and thirst when they have become indifferent to their body. Who else can be their friend who have no friend except God? . . . When God sends down His grace, even poison may become nectar" (Abg. 209). "All the Purānas bear witness as to how God fulfils the desires of His Saints. He has Himself become their Guru, has protected them before and behind, has held them by the hand and shown them the way, and has finally taken them to His heavenly home" (Abg. 472). "Their innermost desires have been fulfilled by God. For God knows the sincerity and earnestness of their desires. Only, the devotees should not be in a hurry, for nothing can avail them when time is out of joint" (Abg. 953). "Those especially who ask nothing of God, and bear disinterested love towards Him, God pursues outright in order that they may ask something of Him. He waits upon them as an attendant, is afraid of sitting down before them, and sacrifices Himself wholly for their sake" (Abg. 1411).

"And when the Saints have sat down quietly in their places and have meditated on Him, . . . God on His part has been kind and has fulfilled their desires unasked" (Abg. 672). "He has lived with His devotees without minding their caste and creed. He has eaten with Vidura, the son of a concubine, has dyed skins with Rohidāsa, has woven silken clothes with Kabīra, has sold flesh with Sajana, has tilled the garden with Sāmvatā, has carried away dead cattle with Chokhā, has gathered cow-dung with Janābāī, . . . has moved the wall of Jñānadeva, has been the charioteer of Arjuna, . . . has been the door-keeper of Bali, has warded off the debt of Ekanātha, . . . has taken poison for Mirābāī, has been a Mahāra for Dāmājī, has borne earthen pots with Gorā, . . . and has been waiting to this day for Puṇḍalīka on a brick in Paṇḍharapūr" (Abg. 2047). "He has done great miracles for His Saints. He has turned the temple at Āvaṇḍhyā, has cashed the cheque of Narasī Mehtā, . . . has brought to life the dead child of the Potter" (Abg. 3250). God's office for the Saints has been truly remarkable.

XIV. SAINTS AND THEIR CHARACTERISTICS

Real Saints are Difficult to Find

71. The Saints, however, can rarely be met with. "We see many people calling themselves Saints. But who will believe everybody who calls himself a Saint? Sainthood is discovered only in times of trial. The brooks overflow in times of rain; but when the rainy season has passed, not a drop of water can be found in them. Pebbles look like diamonds only so long as a hammer has not tested them" (Abg. 251). "Many people indeed look like Saints, but they are not Saints. Saints are not those who can compose poetry. Saints are not those who are relatives of Saints. . . . Saints are not those who hold the sounding gourd in their hands, or those who wear rags. Saints are not those who engage themselves in a sermon, or those who narrate mythological stories. Saints are not those who recite the Vedas, or those who perform caste duties. Saints are not those who go to a pilgrimage, or to a forest. Saints are not those who wear garlands and white marks on their body. Saints are not those who besmear their body with ashes. Until the consideration of the body is at an end," says Tukā, "nobody can become a Saint by engaging himself in Samsāra" (Abg. 1588). "Pseudo-saints are like women, who show counterfeit pregnancy by creating a hollow of clothes under their wearing garment. They neither have milk in their breasts, nor a child in their wombs. Ultimately, the world finds them to be merely barren women" (Abg. 2244). Tukā indeed is not like the pseudo-saints. "He knows no wiles by which people may be deceived. . . . He can never show any miracles. He has no long list of disciples with him. He does not go on instructing people who do not care for his advice. He is not the head of a Maṭha. . . . He does not make the King of Ghosts work out his bidding. . . . He is not a philosopher who can argue about trifles. He does not whirl round himself a fire-brand in ecstasy. He does not count beads and thus try to influence people about him. He is no Tāntrist who can use the black art for his purposes. Tukā indeed is not like these mad people who carve out a home for themselves in hell" (Abg. 137). Tukārāma tells us that the greatness of Saints cannot be estimated unless one has become a Saint himself. "Verily difficult of understanding is the greatness of a Saint. Wordy knowledge is of no use there. Howsoever large the quanity of milk which a cow or a she-buffalo might give, can she be compared to the Milch-cow of heaven? We can know the greatness of Saints only when we have become like them," says Tukā (Abg. 676). "The Saints incarnate in this world only in order to uplift the unholy, and to increase happiness and devotion to God. Just as a sandal tree can make other trees fragrant, similarly, a Saint makes other people holy in this world" (Abg. 2451).

Characteristics of Saints

72. The first characteristic of a saint is that he is calm and tranquil, and bears like a diamond the buffets of misfortune. "That diamond alone fetches immense value, which remains unbroken under the travail of a hammer. That gem is costly, which, when it comes into contact with a piece of cloth, does not allow it to be burnt by fire.

That man alone is a great saint," says Tukā, "who bears imperturbably the buffets of the world" (Abg. 25). In fact, there is no other external mark of God-realisation except that a man be tranquil under God. "Thou tellest people that thou art God, and yet hast an inner desire for sense. Thou tellest others the sweetness of nectar, while thou art thyself being famished to death. That man alone," says Tukā, "is equal to God, who is absolutely tranquil under the power of Self-realisation" (Abg. 1193). In the second place, a Saint cares not for the evil talk of the world, when he is following the ways of God. "The devotee of God is dear to God alone. He cares not for others. He cares for no friend or companion. People might call him a madman. . . . He lives in forests, and woods, and in uninhabited places. When he besmears his body with ashes after having taken a bath, people look at him and blame him. When he sits alone to himself with a rosary of Tuḷasī beads on his neck, people ask—Why is it that he has been sitting apart? He is not ashamed of singing, nor of sitting anywhere he pleases, and his parents and brothers abuse him for his manner. His wife calls him names, and says that is would have been better if that impotent fellow had died. . . . He alone can achieve the end of life," says Tukā, "who has turned his back away from the world" (Abg. 1185). Thirdly, miracle-mongering, says Tukā, is no test of spirituality. "He who can tell what is going to happen in future, or can give news of the past and the present—I am entirely weary of these fellows! I do not like to see them. Those who follow after powers, and try to make reality square with their words—these, will go to hell after their merit is exhausted" (Abg. 948). It is only the unfortunate who care for the knowledge of the past, present and future. "We, the servants of the Lord, should only meditate upon Him in our mind, and allow fortune to take its own course. When a man keeps a shop of miracle-mongering, God keeps away from him. Bad indeed is Samsāra, but worse is the pursuit of power" (Abg. 638). In the fourth place, says Tukārāma, a servant of God is afraid of none. He entertains no fear of any person or thing. "He who has seen God stands as it were on an eminence. He who has seen God is afraid of none. He who has seen God will ask what he likes of God Himself. He who has seen God knows that God will fulfil all his wishes. He who has seen God knows that God cuts off his inner desires as with a pair of scissors" (Abg. 1267). And thus the Saint is not afraid of death at all. "The messengers of Death will run away when they see flocks of Saints. When the Saints come, Demons and Death shake with mortal fear. The whole earth rejoices by the spiritual ensign of the Saints, and Death takes to his heels when he sees that powerful army" (Abg. 1535). The fifth characteristic of a Saint is his absolute equality. "A Saint devotes himself entirely to the happiness of others. He worships God in helping his fellow-beings. When one troubles others, we may say, he hates God. . . . This alone is Saint-hood," says Tukā; "for, by this, man makes himself equal to the Self" (Abg. 2972). For such a Saint, no enemy can exist; because he himself has no feeling of enmity towards another. "To us there are neither friends nor foes; for wherever I see, I see the vision of God. Wherever I cast my eyes, I see God Pāṇḍuraṅga and Rakhumāī, Rādhā, and Satyabhāmā. We have lost all shame and all anxiety, and happiness is wallowing at our feet. We, who are the sons of God, have become the fondlings of people in the world" (Abg. 1357). A Saint, says Tukārāma, is known by his compassion to humanity. "Those who are unhappy or sorrow-stricken, a Saint calls his own. Such a man alone deserves to be a Saint. God is present only with him. His mind is as soft as butter. The compassion which he feels for his son, he also feels for his servants and maids. It is needless to say," says Tukā, "that such Saints are incarnations of God" (Abg. 201). Also, in such a Saint, opposite qualities like extreme mildness and extreme severity are to be simultaneously found. "The servants of God are softer than wax and harder than a diamond. They are dead though living, and awake though sleeping. They will fulfil the desires of all, and give them whatever they desire. . . . They will be more affectionate than parents, and work greater wrong than enemies. Nectar cannot be sweeter, and poison more bitter than these Saints,"says Tukā (Abg. 586). Sixthly, a Saint never leaves his spiritual practice in spite of calamities. "He alone is a servant of

God, who loves God wholly. He cares for nothing else except God. When calamities befall him, he sticks to his spiritual practice" (Abg. 214). He is prepared even to sacrifice his life for spirituality. "Sainthood cannot be purchased in a market-place, nor can it be acquired by wandering in woods and forests. Sainthood cannot be bought by large quantities of wealth, nor can it be found in the upper and the nether worlds. Sainthood can be acquired," says Tukā, "only at the cost of life. He, who is not prepared to sacrifice his life, should not brag of spirituality" (Abg. 677). Finally, the Saint goes beyond all dualities like sin and merit, death and life, and so on. "No room has now been left for sin and merit, or for happiness and misery. . . . Death has occurred during life and the distinction between Self and not-Self has disappeared. . . . There is now no room for caste or colour or creed, or for truth and untruth. . . . When the body has been sacrificed to God," says Tukā, "all worship has been accomplished" (Abg. 3171). "The Saint has also gone beyond the influence of all sorts of actions: he cannot do any actions which can bear any fruit. God has taken the place of action, and has filled the inside and the outside of the Saint. . . . Indeed, there has now remained no distinction," says Tukā, "between God and the Devotee" (Abg. 155). And, "if God is now to be found anywhere, He is to be found in such Saints and not in the images. If one goes to a place of pilgrimage, one can find only stones and water. But in the Saints, one finds God. . . . Places of pilgrimage are useful to those who have devotion. In the company of the Saints, on the other hand, even rustics become good," says Tukā (Abg. 89).

The Spiritual Power of the Saints

73. The spiritual power of Saints is indeed very great. "The sun and the lamp and the diamond show things which are visible. But the Saints show things which are invisible. . . . Parents are the cause of birth. But Saints are the cause of the cessation of birth. . . . It is for these reasons," says Tukā, "that we should go to the Saints unasked, and cling to their feet" (Abg. 722). The Saints have indeed kept their shops open, and give to whomsoever goes to them with any desire. The Saints indeed are generous, and their treasure cannot be emptied. Those who beg will have their heart's content, and yet a large remainder will be left for others. When a bag is filled with God," says Tukā, "it can never be emptied" (Abg. 1866). "Various people have taken away the contents of this mine, and yet it has never been emptied. The Saints of bygone ages have left this treasure for us. By the power of his devotion, Puṇḍalīka brought it to the notice of the world. Tukārāma was a poor beggar there, and received only a small quantity of it" (Abg. 2981).

The Saints' Influence Upon Others

74. So far as their influence upon others is concerned, we may say that the Saints spread happiness all round. The very dust of their feet, says Tukārāma, brings happiness to people. "Immense pleasure is derived from the feet of the Saints. It is for this reason that people live at their feet. One cannot even so much as stir from that place, as all of one's anxieties come to an end. The whole body becomes cool," says Tukā, "when the dust of the Saints' feet touches one's body" (Abg. 2528). "All sin and sorrow depart at the sight of a holy man. No holy place has the power of taking away sin and sorrow. God Himself bows to the pollen of the Saint's feet, and dances when he performs a Kīrtana. The Saint is indeed a boat by which one can cross the ocean of life uncontaminated by the stream of existence" (Abg. 990). "Sinful men must needs take care not to give trouble to the Saints. For thereby they only give invitation to death. The dog barks at the heel of the elephant, but is obliged to turn back in shame. When a monkey teases a lion, it is surely giving invitation to death. Sinful men who tease the Saints will have only their faces blackened," says Tukā (Ab. 2426). Finally, the Saints deprive everybody who comes into contact with them of all his possessions. "They are verily robbers, who on coming to the house, deprive the owner of his clothes and earthen pots. They rob him of everything in his possession, and take it away to a place from which there is no return" (Abg. 1904).

XV. THE IDENTITY OF SAINTS WITH GOD

Establishment of Identity Between God and the Saints

75. The Saints by their perfect morality and devotion raise themselves to the position of the Godhead. Tukārāma tells us that "Gods are Saints, and Saints, Gods. Images are merely the occasional cause of worship. . . . The impersonal God cannot satisfy our wants. But the Devotee satisfies all (Abg. 3993). God and Saint are merely the obverse and the reverse sides of the same spiritual coin. "God has to take on incarnation, and the Devotee engages himself in worldly life. . . . The Devotee derives happiness by God; and God derives happiness in the company of the Devotee. God gives the Saint a form and a name, and the Saint increases His glory. . . . One should surely rest in the belief that the Saint is God, and God the Saint" (Abg. 3324). It is this identity which makes a Saint even enter into a quarrel with God. "Art Thou alone immortal, and am I not immortal? Let us go to the Saints, O God, and have their judgment on this point. Thou hast no name no doubt, but equally have I no name. Thou hast no form no doubt, but equally have I no form. Thou playest as in sport, equally do I play in sport. As Thou art true and false, equally am I true and false," says Tukā (Abg. 1586). Thus it comes about that the distinction between God and the Devotee is an illusion. "We have now come to know Thy real nature. There is neither Saint nor God. There is no seed, how can there be a fruit? Everything is an illusion. Where is merit, and where is sin? I have now seen my own Self. . . . I am celebrating the name of God only for the sake of others, says Tukā" (Abg. 1300). And yet, in a way, God and Saint *are* like seed and tree. "From the seed grows the tree, and from the tree comes the fruit. Thus art Thou and I like seed and tree. The waves are the ocean, and the ocean the waves. Image and reflection have now merged into each other," says Tukā (Abg. 2242). And yet, even though the Saint has attained to identity with God, he manifests a difference for the sake of others. "The devotee alone can know the greatness of a devotee. It is impossible for others to know that greatness. By the power of the great happiness, the Saint knows and yet does not know; he speaks, and yet does not speak. He has become one with God, and yet shows a difference in order that the cause of devotion may prosper. . . . It is only those who have realised God that can understand the meaning of what I say," says Tukā (Abg. 893). Indeed, in order to know God, one has to become God. "It is only he who has become God, that can understand that others are gods. Those who have not known this are only tale-tellers. He who has satisfied his hunger cannot know that others are hungry: he looks upon other people's happiness in the light of his own. What is wanted here," says Tukā, "is experience, and not words" (Abg. 2065).

The Saint Is Even Superior to God

76. And yet in a way the Devotee is even superior to God. "God is required to provide for His creation, the Devotee has no anxiety even to provide for himself. God has to take into account the merits and sins of people: to the Devotee all are equally good. God has to create and to destroy the world; the Devotee is not called upon to undertake that onerous duty. God is always engaged in His work; the Devotee enjoys the satisfaction of not doing anything at all. Does not all this prove that the Devotee is superior to God?" (Abg. 1189). And the Devotee by his power can even rule over God. "Before the power of his devotion, no other power avails. Who can rule God except His devotee? Wherever the Devotee sits, all things come of their own accord, and nobody ever dares to do him wrong" (Abg. 1283). The Saint can even exercise authority over God, as Tukārāma did. "Go to my house with me, O God, and stand still until I place my head on Thy feet. Allow me to embrace Thee, and look at me with compassion. I shall wash Thy feet, and make Thee sit in my mid-house. . . . I shall make Thee eat with me, and Thou darest not refuse. Thou hast hitherto prevented me from knowing the secret. Why may one now be afraid of Thee when one has come to know the truth? By the power of my devotion, I shall now make Thee do whatever I please," says Tukā (Abg. 2582). And God in return will fold His hands before His devotee as He did before Tukā. "What can be lacking to us?" asks Tukā. "All powers have now come to our door. He, who has imprisoned the demons of the world, now folds His hands before us. Him, who has neither name nor form, we have endowed with a name and a form. He, in whom the whole universe is enclosed, is to us now as good as an ant. We have really become more powerful than God," says Tukā, "when we have once set aside all our desires" (Abg. 126).

XVI. TUKĀRĀMA'S PANTHEISTIC TEACHING

A Pantheistic Unification of the Personal and the Impersonal

77. The trend of all this teaching is a final pantheistic unification of the Personal and the Impersonal. The form which is worshipped by outward means, and the form which is experienced by an inner vision, are, according to this teaching, ultimately one. "What the Yogins visualise in their ecstasy is the same as what appears to our physical vision. The form of God, which stands before us with His hands on His waist, is the same as that Impersonal Existence which envelops all, which has neither form nor name, . . . which has neither end, nor colour, nor standing-place; which is familyless, casteless, handless, and footless. The Impersonal shines forth as the Person by the power of devotion," says Tukā (Abg. 320). And all sciences proclaim the universal immanence of God. "The Vedānta has said that the whole universe is filled by God. All sciences have proclaimed that God has filled the whole world. The Purānas have unmistakably taught the universal immanence of God. The Saints have told us that the world is filled by God. Tukā indeed is playing in the world uncontaminated by it like the Sun which stands absolutely transcendent" (Abg. 2877). When such universal presence of God is realised, "who will care for all those paltry stone-deities which, when they are hungry, beg alms for themselves. . . . Why should one care for hospitality from the Maid-servants in the house? The Maid is powerless, and must go to her Mistress to dole out rations of food. The water in a pond can never give satisfaction to a thirsty man. . . . These little deities hide their faces under the red ointment which besmears their bodies. . . . He is a fool who calls them gods. The real God is the universal immanent God. Meditate on Him," says Tukā (Abg. 4074). And it is due to the universal immanence of God that He acts as a thread through all the pearls of existence. He is verily the *vinculum substantiale* of all, and holds all things together. "By our relation to God, the whole world has become ours, as all pearls are threaded on the same string. . . . The happiness and misery of others is reflected in us as the happiness and misery of ourselves is reflected in them" (Abg. 426). It is this experience which makes all people gods. It is this experience which makes a Saint look upon all beings as the incarnations of the immortal Godhead. "Immortal are ye all verily. . . . Think not of your body as your own, and then you will realise the truth of my assertion. Why need fear anything at all, when all things are ours? Believe me," says Tukā, "that all of ye are verily gods" (Abg. 849). And the true Saint is he who having realised the oneness of God, His immanence everywhere, and His ultimate identity with his own self, is enabled to say that there is no God beyond himself. "We should only say," says Tukā, "that there is a God; but should realise in our minds that there is none. Love now meets love, body body. The internal becomes one with the external. . . . The son has now met his parent. An inexpressible vision has been seen, and one now rejoices and is moved to tears" (Abg. 3208). And it is wonderful, says Tukā, that when such a real spiritual experience is within the reach of all, they should carry on their physical life as alone real. "They forget the memory of death. . . . They forget that the body is merely a prey to death. They shut their eyes and grow deliberately blind" (Abg. 2625). "They do not know how the Self is playing with the Self; how the ocean has mingled with the rivers; how space is merged in space. The seed now points to the seed: the leaf and the flower are only an illusion" (Abg. 2692). "God indeed is an illusion. The Devotee is an illusion. Everything is an illusion. Only those who have got this experience," says Tukā, "will come to know the truth of my remark" (Abg. 2524). The unreal Tukā is speaking unreal things with unreal men. Everywhere there is a reign of unreality. "One laughs vainly, and one weeps vainly. . . . Vainly do people say that this is mine, and this is thine. . . . Vainly does a man sing, and vainly does he meditate. Unreality meets unreality. The unreal man enjoys, the unreal man abandons. Unreal is the saint; Unreal is Māyā. The unreal Tukā, with an unreal devotion, speaks unreal things with unreal men" (Abg. 2096). To such heights are we carried by the force of Tukārāma's pantheistic teaching.

XVII. THE DOCTRINE OF MYSTICAL EXPERIENCE

Knowledge as an Obstacle in the Way of Reaching God

78. Tukārāma's mystical experience is absolutely on a par with the experience of those who have preceded him, or those who have followed him. All mystics, it has been said, speak the same language, to whatever country they may belong; and if we collect together the various utterances of Tukārāma on the head of mystical experience, we will find that he is giving vent to the same feelings which have inspired other mystics. "Let us go," he says, "in the wake of those who have gone ahead of us; for they have been wiser than us. . . . Let us gather together this great spiritual wealth. . . . Meditation on the Name of God is alone sufficient to bring to us untold benefits. Life and birth would thus come to an end. Let us kill our individual self," says Tukā, "and go to our original home" (Abg. 13). "In this path, consciousness of knowledge is a great obstacle. A mother indeed ceases to take care of the self-conscious child. When once the pearls are taken out of water, they can never again be resolved into water. When butter has been prepared, it is for all times severed from buttermilk" (Abg. 1705). "Of two children, the mother takes care of the younger one, and admonishes the other. It is consciousness which brings greater responsibility. Both the children are hers, and yet she behaves differently with either. She throws off her elder child, and puts to her breast the younger one when it begins to cry" (Abg. 111). "The cow-herd friends of Kṛishṇa were never conscious of their possession of God, and hence God liked them more than those who boasted of their learning. God turns away from boastful men, by creating in them egoism, difference, and censure" (Abg. 3865). In great humility, therefore, Tukā says merely "Viṭṭhala," "Viṭṭhala," and invites the learned to spit on him. "Tukā indeed is a thoughtless madman, and is given to bragging. He is given to the uttering of the Name of God, Rāma, Kṛishṇa, Hari forever. . . . He finds that the Teacher's knowledge is all-pervading. He listens to nobody, and dances naked in a Kīrtana. He is weary of enjoyments, and wallows in uninhabited places. He cares not for advice, and says Viṭṭhala, Viṭṭhala. People criticise him variously, but he carries on his vocation. Spit on me, O learned men," says Tukā, "for I am without learning" (Abg. 2090).

The Importance of Realisation

79. There is a great deal of difference between an intellectual conviction of God's omnipresence, and a mystical vision of Him. "The Anāhata sound is present in all. But, how can a man get liberation unless he utters the Name of God? God is indeed present in all beings. But nobody has yet been liberated without having seen Him. Knowledge is present in all. But without devotion it is incompetent to take one to Brahman. What is the use of all the different postures in Yoga, unless the ecstatic light shines? Feed not the body," says Tukā, "for by that God could never be found" (Abg. 1187). Tukārāma hates all mythologies. What he wants is spiritual realisation. "I do not want the stories of old," he says. "What is the use of those dry words? I want experience, and nothing else. You talk of knowledge, but I know that you have had no mystical experience. The royal swan can distinguish between water and milk. What is wanted is a true coin, and not a counterfeit one" (Abg. 2277). It is this consideration of the inferiority of all merely intellectual knowledge to mystical realisation that makes the attainment of the end a very difficult task. "The blossom may be infinite, but the fruits are few. Fewer still are the fruits that ripen, and fewest come unspoilt from the fruit-store. Rare indeed is the man who has the satisfaction of having reached the end. . . . Rare is the man who attains to victory in the midst of blazing swords. I shall call him my companion, says Tukā, who has been able to reach the end" (Abg. 752).

The Grace of God

80. The greatest help, however, to realisation comes from the grace of God. Without the grace of God, says Tukārāma, no Sādhana is of any avail. "What is the use of all Sādhanas?" asks Tukā. "God's form will appear before us only if He takes compassion upon us. All our efforts would be of no use, unless they reach the final tranquillity" (Abg. 3165). "If only God wills, then alone can He endow us with spiritual vision. We need not go anywhere, nor bring anything from anywhere. If only God wills, these eyes shall have a spiritual vision, and our egoism shall disappear" (Abg. 3139). It was thus that God was attained by the Sages of old. "Śuka and Sanaka have borne witness that Parīkshit was able to attain to God in a week. Remember God's Name with all speed, and then God cannot hold Himself back. He will hasten as He did for the sake of Draupadī, and come ahead of

His swift-winged Eagle. He cannot contain His love, and will run to the devotee's help" (Abg. 102).

Psychology of Mysticism

81. Tukārāma's contribution to the Psychology of Mysticism is very clever and profound. He tells us, in the first place, that while we are contemplating God, both body and mind are entirely transformed. "When the Self has been transformed in God, and when the mind has been suffused in illumination, the whole of creation looks divine, and all of a sudden the influx of God fills the whole world" (Abg. 3133). Thus Tukārāma directs all Saints to sing the praises of God alone. "If I were to utter the praises of anybody except Thyself, let my tongue fall down. If my mind longs to think of anybody except Thyself, let my head break in twain. If my eyes have a passion for seeing anything except Thee, let them become blind at that very moment. If my ears refuse to hear Thy praise, they would be as good as useless. My very life would have no *raison d'être*," says Tukā, "if I were to be oblivious of Thy presence even for a moment" (Abg.

260). All the senses therefore, Tukārāma advises us, should be directed to the contemplation of God. "Your hands and feet must work for the sake of God. You have speech to utter His praise, and ears to hear His greatness. You have eyes to see His form. Blind men, and deaf men, and dumb men, and lame men, have hitherto gone without having an opportunity of serving God. He, who keeps himself in his house by setting it on fire, will soon cease to exist. Now at least," says Tukā, "be awake, and do what is conducive to the highest happiness" (Abg. 511). "Let all the senses quarrel with one another," says Tukā, "for the enjoyment of God. My various organs are now at war with one another. My ears say that my tongue has been pleased. My hands and feet are pining for the service of God. My eyes are experiencing the dearth of His vision. Other senses are quarrelling with my ears, because they hear the praises of God, and with my speech, because it utters His greatness. . . . If Thou art kind, O God, create such a confusion among my senses" (Abg. 2593). "Let all the emotions be now transformed for the sake of God. Thou followest evanescent things. Why dost thou not follow God? As thou lovest another person, why dost thou not love God? Thou hast affection for thy son. Why dost thou not have that same affection towards God? Thou lovest thy wife, who ultimately robs thee of everything that thou hast got. Why dost thou not have that same tender affection for God? Thou worshippest thy parents in the consciousness of their obligation. Why dost thou not regard the obligation of God? Thou art afraid of other men. Why art thou not afraid of God? Dost thou suppose that thou hast come to life in vain?" (Abg. 2511). People, says Tukā, are ashamed of uttering the Name of God. "Bring Shame to the temple," he says. "We shall put herself to shame. I ring this cymbal in the Name of God. Give no shelter to Shame. This witch has spoilt good ways, and has taken people by the path of destruction. She shows herself off among men, and is crafty and mean. Bring her to the temple; we shall make her ashamed" (Abg. 2604). People do not experience tears in the contemplation of God, says Tukā. "Unless tears come out of our eyes in the contemplation of God, we cannot be said to have true devotion. Tears indeed are an index of love towards God" (Abg. 57). Also, spiritual contemplation has the value of stilling the mind. "Experience leads to experience. The mind gets stilled on the feet of God. The dross is burnt in the fire of God, and from the gold comes out a new ornament. Blissfulness alone remains. We conquer the worlds," says Tukā, "by being the servants of God" (Abg. 783). And this beatification leads on to final spiritual silence. "Why now waste words? Whatever had been desired has been obtained. A union has been effected between Name and Form. Vain words have come to an end. As a dumb man eats sugar, so the mytic enjoys beatification. What now follows," says Tukā, "is utter spiritual silence" (Abg. 262).

The Manifold Vision of God

82. The immediate effect of carrying on a spiritual life is that the devotee is endowed with a new vision. "Red, and white, and black, and yellow, and other variegated colours fill the new spiritual vision. The spiritual collyrium opens out a divine eye. The vagaries of the mind stop automatically. Space and time cease to have any existence. The Self illumines the whole Universe. Physical existence comes to an end. The identity of God and Self takes place. 'I am Thou' is the spiritual experience which emerges in a state of beatification" (Abg. 3248). "When God shows Himself to the saints, the very monads are filled with light. Only those who have control over their senses," says Tukā, "can understand this. This is what is called spiritual collyrium" (Abg. 495). "The mind should be placed on the feet of God. When it has been so placed, we should not lift it up again; for, God's form will melt away if it be moved by a little. God will now embrace the Saint, and will keep him beside Himself" (Abg. 1805). "And the form of God will be seen as pervading the whole universe. Society and solitude will cease to have any difference. Wherever a devotee looks, he will see God and His spouse. In the woods as in the city, all space will be pervaded by God. Happiness and sorrow will be at an end, and the Saint will dance in joy" (Abg. 24). "He will dance along with his spiritual companions. . . . All peace, forbearance, and compassion, he will find in the Name of God. Why should he now grow indifferent to his body, when he has once found by it the stream of nectar? Why should he long for solitude? He would find that great bliss now in society. In fact, he would experience that God is constantly moving with him" (Abg. 470). And God indeed moves after the holy man. "His body is holy, and his speech holy. He utters constantly the Name of God. By meditating on the Saint, even sinful men will be relieved of their sin. God follows him, desiring to purify himself by the pollen of his feet. What can now be lacking to a Saint with whom God is ever present? We can now see the triple spiritual confluence of the Saint, God, and the Name" (Abg. 989). And if the Saint travels, God also travels with him. "Blissful in listening to the divine Kīrtana, God lives in the company of the Saint. A Saint like Nārada moves travelling and singing the Name of God, and God moves along with him. Nārada sings devotional music and God listens to it. God indeed loves no other thing so much as His own Kīrtana" (Abg. 3026). "God even dances before the singing Saint. That incarnate bliss, the form of God, stands in the courtyard of the devotee. The Saint does not care for liberation. Liberation cares for the Saint" (Abg. 301). "As the Saint sleeps and sings, God stands up to hear the song; as the Saint sits down to sing God's Name, God nods with pleasure; as the Saint stands up and utters the Name of God, God dances before him; as the Saint moves on his way singing the name of the Lord, God stands before him, and behind him. God indeed loves His Kīrtana as nothing else, and, for the sake of His Name, comes to the Saint's rescue at all times" (Abg. 1032). "God raises His hand and asks the Saint to choose whatever he likes. God is omniscient, God is generous, God is verily the father, and He supplies whatever the Saint wants" (Abg.1403). "He does all the Saint's work unasked. He stands pent up inside his heart, and He stands outside with a beautiful form. He looks at His devotee's face in order that he may ask something of Him. Whenever the Saint desires anything, He fulfils it at once. But the Saint rests his mind on the feet of God, and asks for nothing" (Abg. 1343). Finally, the Saint becomes so unified with

God, that it is impossible to distinguish between God and Saint. "Embrace meets embrace. Body is unified with body. The mind refuses to turn back in its enjoyment of God. Words mix with words. Eyes meet eyes. And as the Gopīs of old became merged in God, so does the Saint become one with Him in his inner contemplation" (Abg. 1614).

The Life After God-attainment

83. The Saint now goes about telling people that God has risen. He asks them to keep awake and arise from their sensual sleep. "Awake and arise," he says to the people, "God has arisen. All the saints have been merged in happiness. The universe is full of spiritual joy. Now beat the cymbals, and blow the trumpets. Let all musical instruments make a chorus of God. Fold up your hands before God; look at God's face; and rest your head on God's feet. Tell God your sorrow," says Tukā, "and ask of Him whatever you want" (Abg. 4044). "To a man who has become such a friend of God, the very creepers in the court-yard are as wish-trees. As he moves on his way, the very stones become wish-jewels. His very babbling is more significant," says Tukā, "than the teaching of the Vedānta" (Abg. 2157). "And the Saint has undergone all this trouble in order that the final day might bring him the spiritual crown. His mind now rests in peace, and his desires are at an end. He wonders how he has had to wade through such a laborious process. But he is satisfied that it has at last landed him in the sure possession of God. He has now married Liberation, and will live with her a few happy days" (Abg. 787).

XVIII. SPIRITUAL ALLEGORIES

The Allegory of the Crop

84. Following the example of spiritual teachers like Ekanātha who had gone before him, Tukārāma makes free use of allegories for the expressions of his spiritual ideas. In order to explain what we mean, we shall select three or four out of a number of allegories employed by Tukārāma. We shall first take the allegory of the Crop. We are asked by Tukārāma "to rear the crop of God's name on the land which has come in our possession. There is neither any Government assessment here, nor any external oppression. . . . No thieves can come and attack this crop, and yet he who is anxious as to how this crop will grow is a fool. . . . The crop of God's love is vast and wide, and nobody has space enough to garner it" (Abg. 3327). "The keeper of the crop who does not guard it will ultimately lose all his grain, because the birds will come and feed upon it. . . . Those who deliberately shut their eyes in broad day-light will fall into a ditch. How can a man who keeps a barren cow be able to get milk and ghee from her?" (Abg. 3328). "Guard the four corners of the crop, and rest not until the crop is reaped from the fields. Let the Name of God serve as a stone in the sling of thy breath, so that the birds in the form of desires will fly away. Blow the fire of Self-realisation, and keep awake. . . .When you have gathered the corn, hand over to the elements their portions from the stock, and enjoy the rest" (Abg. 3329).

The Allegory of the Dish

85. Another allegory which Tukārāma employs is the allegory of the Dish. We are told to blow the chaff from the wheat, the Body from the Soul. Let the pestle of discrimination stop working when the wheat is separated from the chaff. The bangles in the form of the mystic sounds will now make a noise, and let the Name of God be sung in tune with the sounds. . . . And when the Self will appear to us as in a mirror, at that moment the spiritual dish may be considered to be ready" (Abg. 3712).

The Fortune-teller

86. Thirdly, we have barely to mention the allegory of the Fortune-teller, who comes and says that "he who says that all this is truth will go to hell. He who says that all this is a lie will enjoy happiness. Sleep therefore in your own places and believe in the thief who robs peoples' hearts. A chaste woman is handed over to the possession of five, and when she engages herself with the Supreme Person, she will enjoy happiness" (Abg. 3981).

The Supreme Power as Goddess

87. Finally, we note Tukārāma's allegorical representation of the Supreme Power as

Goddess. "Rajas and Tamas are burnt as incense before that Goddess. The ram of mind is killed with a fist, and in the rumbling of the Anāhata sound, the deity takes possession of the body and frees Tukā from disease" (Abg. 3958). "This deity," says Tukā, "dances along with the Saints. She is with you already; but you have mistaken her place. She gives eyes to the blind, and feet to the lame, and she makes the barren woman give birth to a child. Thus does that deity fulfil all desires" (Abg. 3959). "That deity lives on the banks of the Bhimā at Paṇḍharapūr. Call for her by a thousand names. . . . When the demon teased Prahlāda, she came out at once in all her fierceness. She helped Vasudeva, when his seven children were killed by the demon. She helped the Pāṇḍavas when they were wandering like madmen. She runs to the succour whenever her name is sung. She is verily our mother," says Tukā. "Why need we any longer fear the messengers of Death?" (Abg. 3964). "This deity has now taken possession of me, and refuses to leave me. If you want to dispossess me of her, take me to the banks of the Chandrabhāgā, and place me at the feet of Viṭṭhala; otherwise, there is no hope of life for me" (Abg. 3966).

XIX. THE WORLDLY WISDOM OF TUKĀRĀMA

Tukārāma's Worldly Wisdom

88. The piercing insight which Tukārāma shows in the affairs of the world is extremely remarkable. Having penetrated the heart of reality, it was not difficult for him to understand the affairs of the world. We shall cite here a few illustrations to show what extraordinary insight he had in the affairs of the world. He tells us, in the first place, how a woman's beauty is the cause of sorrow. "Give me not the company of women," he says, . . . "for by them I forget God's worship, and my mind goes beyond my control. A sight of them is spiritual death, and their beauty is the cause of hardship. Even if Fire were to become a Saint," says Tukā, "he would be contaminated by their influence" (Abg. 3347). He tells us how "people avoid the sight of Saints, and look upon another man's wife with great regard. They become weary of the words of Saints;

but their ears are satisfied when they hear the words of women. They sleep while the Kīrtana is being performed; while they are fully awake when women are being described. Be not angry with me," says Tukā, "for I am only describing human nature" (Abg. 3237). Then, Tukārāma goes on to tell us that "real worth can never be hidden. One need not call together the different trees in a forest, and ask them whether the sandal tree has sweet scent. Real worth, though latent, cannot remain hidden. The Sun never orders his rays that they should awake people. The cloud of itself makes the peacocks dance with joy. It is impossible," says Tukā, "to hide real worth" (Abg. 150). On the other hand, Tukārāma tells us that a counterfeit coin can never fetch any price. "A coin of copper can never fetch any price even if it is taken from place to place. The Good and the Old have no respect for the counterfeit. Pebbles shine like diamonds, but the connoisseur knows how to distinguish the one from the other. A painted pearl is never so valuable as a real pearl. Our mind tells the real worth of things. There is no use mincing matters," says Tukā

(Abg. 3146). Then, Tukārāma tells us that in this world smallness is preferable to greatness. "Make me small, O God, like an ant; for the latter gets sugar to eat. A great elephant is subjected to a goad. Those that stand high have many blasts to shake them; and if they fall, they shatter themselves to pieces" (Abg. 744). Smallness offers no occasion for rivalry to anything. "When the great flood sweeps away forests, the small grass subsists. The waves of an ocean cross past us if we humble ourselves down. If we hold a man by his legs," says Tukā, "he will have no power over us" (Abg. 745). Then, Tukārāma tells us, that, under God, as under a Wish-tree, we should ask only for good things. "For the Wish-tree will yield anything that may be desired; and if we entertain good desires, good things will accrue; while if we entertain evil desires, ruin will be our lot" (Abg. 1381). Then, Tukārāma tells us how an ignorant man engages himself in devotion. "An ignorant man desires wealth and not knowledge. An ignorant man has no desire to see God. An ignorant man looks for the fruits of action. An ignorant man is prevailed upon by his senses. Burn the face of such ignorant people by a fire-brand," says Tukā; "for they only increase the ignorance in the world" (Abg. 3150). "There is a very great difference," says Tukā, "between seeming and real affection. What seems is not reality. A shepherd used to attend the sermon of a priest, and he was so much moved by hearing the sermon, that he shed tears in seeming sorrow. People supposed that he was weeping for devotion. But what moved him to tears was really a different thing altogether. The priest once asked the shephered why he was weeping, and the shepherd pointed to the two horns and feet, saying 'I am put in mind of my dead ram when I hear your voice. Thus it is that your sermon moves me to tears.' Seeming affection," says Tukā, "is not real affection" (Abg. 91). Tukārāma then descants upon the uselessness of desire. "Man need only care for a seer of rice. Why need he waste words for other things? . . . His space is measured, which is just three and a half cubits. Why should he aspire after more land? To forget God," he says, "is to put ourselves into all sorts of trouble" (Abg. 1326). Those who live in glass-houses, says Tukā, should not throw stones. "What is the use of the man who scratches the breasts of his own mother? A man who blames the Vedas is merely a Chaṇḍāḷa. Where can we live if we set our house on fire? People are sunk in illusion, and nobody knows the truth," says Tukā (Abg. 793). Tukārāma next tells us that we must succumb to the power of Fate. "By fate, we obtain wealth. By fate, we obtain honour. Why dost thou waste thyself in vain? By fate, a man gets misery. By fate, a man is able to satisfy his hunger. Knowing this, Tukārāma does not complain of anything" (Abg. 2071). "An evil man," says Tukā, "is like a washerman. We are obliged to these washermen for washing away our faults. By the soap of their words, they take away our dirt, without charging us anything for it. They are coolies who work for nothing, and take our burden in vain. They carry us to the other side of the ocean of life," says Tukā, "while they themselves go to hell" (Abg. 1122). Tukārāma supposes that "an evil-talker must have been either a washer-man or a barber in his former birth. His words scratch like a razor. His mouth is like a cleansing vessel. . . . He voluntarily takes on himself the business of washing the faults of others," says Tukā (Abg. 1621). As regards initiation of disciples by a Teacher, Tukārāma tells us that a man should distribute his words in a general way like rain. For if he were to make a disciple, half the sins of his disciple would accrue to him. . . . "We should never adopt a son," says Tukā. "We should not sow on a rock. . . . We should talk about private things with the Saints. We should behave with our wife as with a maid-servant. . . . We should see what is pure and what is impure, and never accept anything that would involve us in a loss" (Abg. 1573). "We should instruct others," says Tukā, "only as they deserve. We should place only as much burden upon others as they could bear. What wisdom is there in covering an ant with an elephant's cloth? A clever huntsman is he," says Tukā, "who employs nooses, and nets, and axes, as occasion requires" (Abg. 2460). Tukārāma next warns us not to live continually in the company of the Saints. "By living always in their company, we shall remember their faults; and when we remember their faults, our merit would come to an end. We should bow to the Saints from a distance, says Tukā, and should think of them respectfully" (Abg. 2587). At the fair of life, says Tukā, we should purchase only those things which would bring no loss. "Purchase not goods which would involve you in a loss. Call to your help the spiritual connoisseur, and think of the ultimate benefit. Whatever glitters, says Tukā, is not gold" (Abg. 1398). "We should never reveal the secret," says Tukā, "to anybody. For if we were to reveal the secret, people will run after us for nothing. They would never take to heart anything which we might teach them. Hence, unless they have Experience of their own, no words of ours would be of any avail" (Abg. 818). Finally, Tukārāma has no belief in omens, as the generality of mankind would have. "A true omen," says Tukā, "is the vision of God. When one remembers God, all benefits will necessarily accrue. By meditating on the Name of God, all speech will become holy, and the quarters full of auspiciousness" (Abg. 961).

CHAPTER 3

General Review

Three Points About Tukārāma's Mysticism

If we now review Tukārāma's Mystical Career and Teaching as a whole, we shall find that he supplies us with a typical illustration of what we have called Personalistic Mysticism. Tukārāma exhibits all the doubts and the disbeliefs, the weaknesses and the sufferings, the anxieties and the uncertainties, through which every aspiring soul must pass before he can come into the life of light, spirit and harmony. There is no other instance in the whole galaxy of the Maratha Saints, barring perhaps Nāmadeva, which can be regarded as illustrative of this human element which we find in Tukārāma. Jñānadeva is a Saint who appears to us from the beginning to the end of his spiritual career as a full-fledged Saint, a Saint not in the making but one already made. It is only rarely that we find in Jñānadeva and Rāmadāsa and other saints the traces of a hazard towards the infinite life, which they must realize as the goal of their spiritual career. In Tukārāma, on the other hand, we find these traces from the beginning to the end of his spiritual career. Jñānadeva is a light that dazzles too much by its brilliance. Tukārāma's light is an accommodative, steady, incremental light which does not glitter too much, but which soothes our vision by giving it what it needs. It is for this reason that we say that the humanistic and personalistic element in Tukārāma is more predominant than in any other Saint. (2) A second question that arises about Tukārāma is whether we may regard him as having been influenced by Christianity. Mr. Murray Mitchell has no hesitation in saying that Tukārāma must be regarded as having been definitely influenced by Christian doctrine, inasmuch as the violence of the Portuguese in India in propagating their religious views must have attracted the attention of the Marathas to the Christian religion, as well as because we find in Tukārāma's life and teaching too much of a similarity to Christ's life and teaching. Dr. Macnicol gives an alternative, telling us that if Tukārāma could not be supposed as having been influenced by Christianity, he must at least be supposed as a remarkable instance of a *mens naturalter Christiana.* Mr. Edwards is more humble and says that his judgment must incline only in the latter direction (p. 282). To our mind, it appears that these are useless attempts to explain the parallelism between Christ and Tukārāma, which could best be explained on the hypothesis of a common mystical experience. All mystics of all ages have spoken almost the same language, and it is no wonder that in Tukārāma we find the reminiscences of Christ's life and thought. In this connection, we must prize very highly the attempt which Mr. Edwards has made in presenting the life and utterances of Tukārāma in Biblical fashion. Thus, for example, if we were to read the account which he gives of Tukārāma's ascension to heaven, we would think as if we are reading a Biblical passage. It were much to be wished that some day these students of Tukārāma were to present his Abhaṅgas to the world in Biblical terminology. But, if, for this reason, they venture to point out that Tukārāma ever knew anything of Christianity or was influenced by Christian doctrine, it would be, as the Maratha proverb goes, like extracting oil from sand. Even to-day, if we consider how very little even the most cultured minds of India know of Christianity, we might not wonder if a rustic saint like Tukārāma, in days of old, when no Christianity had ever penetrated the Mahārāshṭra, knew next to nothing about Christianity. And, as regards the judgment that Tukārāma's teaching is to be prized only so far as it complies with the teaching of Christ, we have only to remember that the teachings of both are to be valued only so far as they conform to a universal mystical experience. Hinduism cannot be tested by reference to the Christian ideal, as Christianity itself cannot be tested by reference to the Hindu ideal. Both Hinduism and Christianity must be tested according to the dictates of a universal mystical religion, which must absorb them both. (3) Finally, when people like Dr. Macnicol cannot understand how Tukārāma could be claimed both by theists and pantheists as an exponent of their views, and when they wonder that that inconsistency could be explained only by saying that Tukārāma was a poet, or that he was a Hindu (*Psalms of the Maratha Saints*, p. 21), they entirely ignore the fact that Tukārāma was a mystic, and that he was neither merely a poet nor merely a Hindu. Tukārāma was verily a citizen of the world, and for that matter, a citizen of the spiritual world. The discrepancies that we meet with in Tukārāma are not an outcome of his "ignorance of the divine dynamic" as Mr. Edwards puts it, but they are due to the fact that Tukārāma was a pilgrim who was wandering in a lonely and helpless world, and that it was not until he saw God that his words could be words of certainty and reality for himself, and of assurance and comfort for others. It was only when he went into the kingdom of God that he could see from aloft into the world below, and give them a message which they could not understand in their ignorance, but which was nevertheless real, because it was a definite echo of the majestic voice of God.